The Crisis of the
European Union

Jürgen Habermas

THE CRISIS OF THE EUROPEAN UNION

A Response

Translated by Ciaran Cronin

polity

First published in German as *Zur Verfassung Europas.*
Ein Essay © Suhrkamp Verlag Berlin 2011

This English edition © Polity Press, 2012
Reprinted 2012

Polity Press
65 Bridge Street
Cambridge CB2 1UR, UK

Polity Press
350 Main Street
Malden, MA 02148, USA

ISBN-13: 978-0-7456-6242-8

A catalogue record for this book is available from the British Library.

Typeset in 11 on 14 pt Sabon
by Servis Filmsetting Ltd, Stockport, Cheshire
Printed and bound in Great Britain by MPG Books Group Limited

The publisher has used its best endeavours to ensure that the URLs for
external websites referred to in this book are correct and active at the time
of going to press. However, the publisher has no responsibility for the
websites and can make no guarantee that a site will remain live or that the
content is or will remain appropriate.

Every effort has been made to trace all copyright holders, but if any have
been inadvertently overlooked the publisher will be pleased to include any
necessary credits in any subsequent reprint or edition.

For further information on Polity, visit our website: www.politybooks.com

Contents

Contents

Preface

Since 2008 we have been witnessing the laborious learning process of the German federal government as it moves reluctantly in small steps towards Europe. Over the past two-and-a-half years it first insisted on unilateral national responses, only to go on to haggle over rescue parachutes, to send out ambiguous signals and to drag its feet over concessions. Now, finally, it seems to have come to the realization that the ordoliberal dream of voluntary stability criteria to which the budgets of the member states were supposed to conform has failed. The dream of the 'mechanisms' which are supposed to render the process of reaching joint political decisions superfluous and to keep democracy in check has been shattered not only by the differences in economic cultures but above all by the rapidly changing constellations of unpredictable environments. Now all the talk is of the 'construction flaw' of a monetary union that lacks the requisite political steering capacities. There is a growing realization that the European treaties have to be revised; but there is a lack of a clear perspective for the future.

Preface

The plans recently in circulation would confine the joint governance of the seventeen euro states to the circle of the heads of government, thus to a 'core' of the European Council. Since this governing body is not able to make legally binding decisions, reflection is concentrating on the kinds of sanctions to be imposed on 'disobedient' governments. But what is actually being proposed here? Who is supposed to force whom to obey decisions with what content? Now that the rigid stability criteria have been extended and flexibilized into the invocations of the 'pact for Europe', the decisions of the European Council are supposed to expand to cover the broad spectrum of all those policies that could influence the global competitiveness of the national economies that have drifted apart. Thus, the European agreements would intervene in the core domains of the national parliaments, from fiscal and economic policy, through social policy, to education and employment policy. The procedure envisaged seems to be that, in order to ensure the political implementation of all goals agreed upon with their colleagues in Brussels, the heads of government would organize majorities in their respective national parliaments under threat of sanctions. This kind of executive federalism of a self-authorizing European Council of the seventeen would provide the template for a post-democratic exercise of political authority.

As was to be expected, this intergovernmental undermining of democracy is meeting with resistance from two sides. The defenders of the nation state are seeing their worst fears confirmed and are now barricading themselves more than ever behind the façades of state sovereignty, even though these were breached long ago. However, in the current crisis they have lost the support of a business lobby whose interest up to now lay in keeping both the common currency and the common market as free as possible from political interventions. On the other side, the long-mute advocates of the 'United States of Europe' have again found their voice, though with this emphatic conception they frustrate their own goal of first promoting integration in core Europe. For with this proposal the well-founded opposition to the precipitous path to a bureaucratic executive federalism becomes entangled in the hopeless alternative between nation state and European federal state. A vague federalism which fails to negate this false alternative in a clear-cut way is no better.

With my essay on the 'constitution' for Europe – that is, on its current state and its political make-up – I want to show, on the one hand, that the European Union of the Lisbon Treaty is not as far removed from the form of a transnational democracy as many of its critics assume. On the other hand, I want to explain why the construction flaw of the monetary union cannot be rectified without a revision of the treaty. The current plans to coordinate the decisions of the EMU states in major areas of policy call for an extended basis of legitimation. However, the constitutional model of a federal state is the wrong one for such a transnational democracy. Once we come to see the European Union as if it had been created for good reasons by two constitution-founding subjects endowed with equal rights – namely, co-originally by the citizens (!) and the peoples (!) of Europe – the architecture of the supranational but nevertheless democratic political community becomes comprehensible. Thus we need only to draw the correct conclusions from the unprecedented development of European law over the past half-century.

The political elites continue to shy away from the daunting prospect of a revision of the treaty. Presumably this hesitation is not just a matter of opportunistic power interests and a lack of decisive leadership. The economically generated apprehensions are inspiring a more acute popular awareness of the problems besetting Europe and are lending them greater existential significance than ever before. The political elites should embrace this unusual boost in public prominence of the issues as an opportunity and also regard it as a reflection of the extraordinary nature of the current situation. But the politicians have also long since become a functional elite. They are no longer prepared for a situation in which the established boundaries have shifted, one which cannot be mastered by the established administrative mechanisms and opinion polls but instead calls for a new mode of politics capable of transforming mentalities.

I would like to use the means at my disposal to try to remove mental blocks that continue to hinder a transnationalization of democracy. In doing so, I will situate European unification in the long-term context of a democratic legal domestication and civilization of state power. This perspective should make it clear that the pacification of belligerent nations – hence the goal that motivated not only the foundation of the United Nations but also the process of European unification after the Second World War – has created the preconditions for realizing a more far-reaching goal, namely, the construction of political decision-making capabilities beyond the nation states. The time when the constitutionalization of international law was focused exclusively on the goal of pacification, which also marked the beginning of the development of the European Union, is long past. The shattering of neoliberal illusions has fostered the insight that the financial markets – indeed, more generally, the functional systems of world society whose influence permeates national borders – are giving rise to problems that individual states, or coalitions of states, are no longer able to master. This need for regulation poses a challenge for politics as such, politics in the singular, as it were: the *international* community of states must develop into a *cosmopolitan* community of states and world citizens.

The essay on the European constitution is followed by a paper (which has already appeared in an academic journal) which explores the connection between the systematic concept of human rights and the genealogical concept of human dignity. By 'genealogical' is meant that the experiences of violated human dignity foster a militant dynamic of outrage which lends repeated impetus to the hope for a worldwide institutionalization of human rights, however improbable this may be. The prospect of a political constitution for world society loses something of its semblance of utopianism when we recall that the rhetoric and politics of human rights have in fact exercised global effects over the past couple of decades. Already from the days of the French Revolution, the tension-laden distinction between civil and human rights has involved an implicit claim that equal rights for everyone should be implemented on a global scale. This cosmopolitan claim means that the role of human rights must not be exhausted by moral criticism of the injustices prevailing within a highly stratified world society. Human rights rely on finding institutional embodiment in a politically constituted world society.

The three political interventions collected in the appendix can be read as commentaries on the ethnocentric image of Europe which is reflected in the self-centred perception of the reunified Germany.

Jürgen Habermas
Starnberg, September 2011

The Crisis of the European Union in Light of a Constitutionalization of International Law – An Essay on the Constitution for Europe[1]

I Why Europe is now more than ever a constitutional project

In the current crisis, it is often asked why we should continue to cling to the European Union at all, not to mention the old aim of an 'ever closer political Union', now that the original motive of making wars in Europe impossible is exhausted. There is more than one answer to this question. In what follows, I would like to develop a convincing new narrative from the perspective of a

[1] My thanks to Armin von Bogdandy for his detailed support and to Claudio Franzius and Christoph Möllers for their critical advice.

1

constitutionalization of international law[2] which follows Kant in pointing far beyond the status quo to a future cosmopolitan rule of law:[3] the European Union can be understood as an important stage along the route to a politically constituted world society.[4] Admittedly, on the laborious path leading up to the Lisbon Treaty, the

[2] Jochen A. Frowein, 'Konstitutionalisierung des Völkerrechts', in *Völkerrecht und Internationales Recht in einem sich globalisierenden internationalen System: Berichte der Deutschen Gesellschaft für Völkerrecht* 39 (2000): 427–47. Although this perspective is closely associated with German jurisprudence in particular, it suggests itself today above all for political reasons; on this, see the preface in Claudio Franzius, Franz C. Mayer and Jürgen Neyer (eds), *Strukturfragen der Europäischen Union* (Baden-Baden: Nomos, 2010), p. 16. A brilliant analysis of the German-language contribution to the history of international law, which also throws light on the prominent status of the idea of a constitutionalization of international law in German jurisprudence, is offered by Martti Koskenniemi in his essay 'Between coordination and constitution: law as German discipline', in *Redescriptions: Yearbook of Political Thought, Conceptual History and Feminist Theory* (Münster: LIT, 2011).

[3] On this interpretation of Kant, for whom the model of the confederation of states is just a stage in the development towards a more far-reaching integration of peoples, see Ulrich Thiele, 'Von der Volkssouveränität zum Völker(staats)recht: Kant – Hegel – Kelsen: Stationen einer Debatte', in Oliver Eberl (ed.), *Transnationalisierung der Volkssouveränität: Radikale Demokratie diesseits und jenseits des Staates* (Stuttgart: Franz Steiner, 2011), pp. 175–96. There he writes: 'The special treaty which would transfer national sovereign rights to supranational or international bodies for the sake of perpetual peace would have to spring from a "treaty among nations themselves" and not merely from a treaty of factual sovereigns' (p. 179).

[4] I dealt with Kant's idea of cosmopolitan law several times between 1995 and 2005. See Habermas, 'Kant's idea of perpetual peace, with the benefit of two hundred years' hindsight', in *The Inclusion of the Other: Studies in Political Theory*, trans. Ciaran Cronin (Cambridge: Polity, 1998), pp. 165–201; 'Does the constitutionalization of international law still have a chance?', in *The Divided West*, trans. Ciaran Cronin (Cambridge: Polity, 2006), pp. 115–93; 'A political constitution for the pluralist world society?', in *Between Naturalism and Religion*, trans. Ciaran Cronin (Cambridge: Polity, 2008), pp. 312–52.

forces friendly to Europe have been worn down by disputes over such constitutional political questions; but, quite apart from the implications for constitutional law of the European 'economic government' now planned, this perspective recommends itself today for two further reasons. On the one hand, the current debate has become narrowly focused on the immediate expedients for resolving the current banking, currency and debt crisis and as a result has lost sight of the political dimension (1); on the other hand, mistaken political concepts are obstructing our view of the civilizing force of democratic legal domestication, and hence of the promise associated from the beginning with the European constitutional project (2).

(1) The economistic narrowing of vision is all the more incomprehensible because the experts seem to be in agreement on the diagnosis of the deeper reasons for the crisis: the European Union lacks the competences to bring about the necessary harmonization of the national economies whose levels of competitiveness are drifting drastically apart. To be sure, in the short term the current crisis is monopolizing all of the attention.[5] However, this should not lead the actors concerned to forget the underlying construction flaw of a monetary union which lacks the requisite political regulatory capacities at the European level, a flaw which is rectifiable only in the longer term. The 'pact for Europe'

---

[5] The considerable uncertainty in the predictions of the relevant economic expert reports is indicative of how the politicians are dealing with this crisis.

repeats an old mistake: legally non-binding agreements concluded by the heads of government are either ineffectual or undemocratic and must therefore be replaced by an institutionalization of joint decisions with irreproachable democratic credentials.[6] The German government has become the catalyst of a Europe-wide erosion of solidarity because for too long it has shut its eyes to the only constructive expedient, one which even the liberal-conservative *Frankfurter Allgemeine Zeitung* now paraphrases with the laconic formula 'more Europe'. None of the governments concerned has yet demonstrated the necessary courage, and they are all strugging ineffectually with the dilemma posed by the imperatives of the major banks and rating agencies, on the one side, and their fear of losing legitimacy among their own frustrated populations, on the other. Their panic-stricken incrementalism betrays the lack of a more expansive perspective.

Since embedded capitalism has run its course and the globalized markets have been outstripping politics, the OECD countries have found it increasingly difficult to stimulate economic growth while at the same time ensuring social security and a tolerably just distribution of income for the mass of the population. After the exchange rates were allowed to float freely, the OECD countries had temporarily defused this structural problem by accepting rising inflation. When this policy generated excessively high social costs, they chose the alternative expedient of increasingly financing public

---

[6] On this, see my article 'A pact for or against Europe?' below (pp. 127–39 in this volume).

budgets through credit. The statistically well-confirmed trends of the past two decades reveal, however, that there has been an increase in social inequality and status insecurity in most of the OECD countries, even as the governments have covered their need for legitimation through sharp rises in public debt. Now the ongoing financial crisis since 2008 has also blocked the mechanism of incurring public debt. And for the time being it remains unclear how austerity policies imposed from above, which are in any case difficult to push through domestically, can be reconciled with maintaining a tolerable level of social security in the long run. The youth revolts in Spain and Great Britain are a portent of the threat to social peace.

Under these conditions the imbalance between the imperatives of the markets and the regulatory power of politics has been identified as the real challenge. In the euro zone, the vague prospect of an 'economic government' is supposed to revitalize the long since hollowed-out stability pact. Jean-Claude Trichet is calling for a joint finance ministry for the euro zone, though without mentioning the parliamentarization of the corresponding financial policy which would then likewise be required – or taking account of the fact that the range of policies relevant for competitiveness extends far beyond fiscal policy and reaches right into the heart of the budgetary privilege of the national parliaments. Still, this discussion shows that the cunning of economic (un)reason has placed the question of the future of Europe back on the political agenda. Wolfgang Schäuble, the last 'European' of stature in Angela Merkel's cabinet, knows that transferring competences from the national to the European level impinges on questions of democratic legitimation. However, the direct election of a president of the European Union, a proposal of which he is a long-standing advocate, would be nothing more than a fig leaf for the technocratic self-empowerment of a core European Council whose informal decisions would circumvent the treaties.

These models of a special kind of 'executive federalism'[7] currently in circulation reflect the reluctance of the political elites to contemplate replacing the established mode of pursuing the European project behind closed doors with the shirt-sleeve mode of a vociferous, argumentative conflict of opinions within the broad public. Given the unprecedented gravity of the problems, one would expect the politicians to lay the European cards on the table without further delay and to take the initiative in explaining to the public the relation between the short-term costs and the true benefits, and hence the historical importance of the European project. In order to do so, they would have to overcome their fear of shifting public moods as measured by opinion polls and rely on the persuasive power of good arguments. All of the governments involved, and for the time being all of the political parties, are flinching at this step.

---

[7] In his essay 'Föderalismus und Demokratie' (in Armin von Bogdandy and Jürgen Bast (eds), *Europäisches Verfassungsrecht: Theoretische und dogmatische Grundzüge* [Heidelberg: Springer, 2010], pp. 73–120) Stefan Oeter uses this expression in a different sense: 'In the EU system, the bureaucracies of the member states to a large extent evade the controlling functions of their domestic (national) parliaments by shifting the problems to be decided to the level of the Union. But at the European level they are subject to nothing even approximating the same degree of political oversight as in the national constitutional systems' (p. 104).

Many of them are instead pandering to the populism which they themselves have cultivated by obfuscating a complex and unpopular topic. Politics seems to be holding its breath and dodging the key issues at the threshold leading from the economic to the political unification of Europe. Why this panic-stricken paralysis? The familiar 'no *demos*' answer suggests itself from a perspective wedded to the nineteenth century: there is no European people; therefore a political Union worthy of the name is built on sand.[8] To this interpretation I would like to oppose a superior one: the enduring political fragmentation in the world and in Europe is at variance with the systemic integration of a multicultural world society and is blocking progress towards civilizing relations of violence within societies and between states through constitutional law.[9]

(2) I would first like to recall what the civilizing force of democratically enacted law involves by briefly reviewing the precarious relation between law and power. Ever since its inception in the early civilizations, political authority has consistently constituted itself in the form of law. The 'coupling' of law and politics is as old as the state itself. Over thousands of years, law has played an ambivalent role in this regard. It served as a means of

---

[8] In Germany at the time of the reunification of the divided nation, this mood acquired a stimulus that ran counter to the Maastricht Treaty; see, for example, Hermann Lübbe, *Abschied vom Superstaat: Vereinigte Staaten von Europa wird es nicht geben* (Berlin: Siedler, 1994).

[9] Norbert Elias (*The Civilizing Process*, trans. Edmund Jephcott [Oxford, and Cambridge, MA: Blackwell, 1994]) develops the concept of civilization chiefly with a view to the increase in socio-psychological capabilities of self-control during the process of modernization.

organization for an authoritarian mode of government, and for the prevailing dynasties it was simultaneously an indispensable source of legitimation. While the legal system was stabilized by the sanctioning power of state, political authority, in order to be accepted as just, relied in turn on the legitimizing force of a sacred law which it administered. The law and the judicial power of the king derived their sacred aura originally from the connection with the mythical gods and spirits and later from the appeal to religious natural law. But it was only after the medium of law had become detached from the ethos of society in the Roman Empire that it could bring its stubborn orientation to bear and finally produce rationalizing effects by legally channelling the exercise of political authority.[10]

However, political authority first had to be secularized and law had to be positivized throughout before the legitimation of authority could become dependent on the legally institutionalized consent of those subject to authority. Only with this development could that democratic juridification of the *exercise* of political authority which is relevant in the present context begin. For this juridification develops not only a *rationalizing* but also a *civilizing* force insofar as it divests state violence of its authoritarian character and thereby transforms the character of the political as such. As a political theologian, Carl Schmitt viewed this civilizing tendency with suspicion because, by diluting the authoritarian core of

---

[10] Systems theory describes this process in terms of a 'coupling' between the subsystems of law and politics which are differentiated in accordance with specific codes; see Niklas Luhmann, *Law as a Social System*, trans. Klaus A. Ziegert, ed. Fatima Kastner (Oxford: Oxford University Press, 2008).

political rule, it also robbed it of its sacred aura.[11] He conceived of the 'substance' of the 'political' as the ability to assert itself of a legally constituted authority, on which, however, no normative fetters may be placed.

On Schmitt's interpretation, this substance was still able to manifest itself at the beginning of the modern era in the struggle of sovereign states against external and internal enemies. It disintegrated – at first in the domestic sphere – only with the constitutional revolutions of the eighteenth century. The constitutional state transforms private citizens into democratic national citizens; it rejects the notion of 'internal enemies' and treats its adversaries – even the terrorists – exclusively as criminals.[12] Only the relations of the sovereign state to its external environment were temporarily 'spared' the normative fetters of democratic legal domestication.[13] One need not share the associated evaluation in order to appreciate the descriptive force of freeing the concept of the 'political' from the fog of a mystified counter-enlightenment and restricting it to the core meaning of a democratically juridified decision-making and administrative power.

In international relations, it was only after the collapse of the League of Nations and since the end of the Second

---

[11] Heinrich Meier, *The Lesson of Carl Schmitt: Four Chapters on the Distinction between Political Theology and Political Philosophy*, trans. Marcus Brainard (Chicago: University of Chicago Press, 2011).

[12] Carl Schmitt, *The Concept of the Political*, trans. George Schwab (Chicago: University of Chicago Press, 1996).

[13] This provides the context for the polemic waged by Schmitt throughout his life against the penalization of wars of aggression in international law; see Carl Schmitt, *War/Non-War? A Dilemma*, ed. and trans. Simona Draghici (Corvallis, OR: Plutarch Press, 2004).

World War – with the founding of the UN and the beginning of the process of European unification – that a juridification of international relations began which goes beyond the tentative attempts to place restrictions on state sovereignty (at least *in bello*) through international law.[14] The civilizing process that continues in these trends, which have accelerated since the end of the Cold War, can be described under two complementary aspects. The immediate objective of the domestication of international violence is to pacify relations between states; however, by curbing the anarchic competition for power and promoting international cooperation, this pacification also makes it possible to establish new supranational procedures and institutions for political negotiation and decision-making. For it is only through such new transnational steering capabilities that the *social* forces of nature that have been unleashed at the transnational level – i.e. the systemic constraints that operate without hindrance across national borders, today especially those of the global banking sector – can also be tamed.[15]

Of course, to date the evolution of the law has been neither peaceful nor linear. Insofar as we wish to speak of accomplishments in this dimension at all – as Kant did in his day in the light of the consequences of the French Revolution[16] – such accomplishments, or 'progress in

[14] Martti Koskenniemi, *The Gentle Civilizer of Nations: The Rise and Fall of International Law 1870–1960* (Cambridge: Cambridge University Press, 2001).

[15] David Held and Anthony McGrew, *Governing Globalization: Power, Authority, and Global Governance* (Cambridge: Polity, 2002).

[16] In *The Conflict of the Faculties*, Kant speaks of 'an event of our time

Why Europe is now a constitutional project

legality', have always been incidental consequences of class struggles, imperialistic conquest and colonial atrocities, of world wars and crimes against humanity, postcolonial destruction and cultural uprooting. But remarkable innovations appeared on the horizon of such constitutional change. Two of these innovations explain how a transnationalization of popular sovereignty is possible in the shape of a democratic alliance of nation states. On the one hand, nation states subordinate themselves to supranational positive law; on the other hand, the EU citizenry as a whole shares the constitution-building power with a limited number of 'constituting states' which acquire a mandate from their peoples to collaborate in founding a supranational political community.

If one regards the development of the European Union under these aspects, the route to a politically workable and democratically legitimized (core) Europe is by no means blocked. Indeed, with the Lisbon Treaty the longest stage of the journey has already been completed (II). The civilizing role of European unification acquires prominence especially in the light of a more far-reaching cosmopolitanism. In the last part I will take up those trends in international law which began with the prohibition of violence in international law and with the

which demonstrates this moral tendency of the human race'. But it is only a 'mode of thinking of the spectators which reveals itself *publicly* in this game of great revolutions' and which shows a predisposition 'to hope for progress toward the better'. In Immanuel Kant, *Religion and Rational Theology*, trans. and ed. Allen W. Wood and George Di Giovanni (Cambridge: Cambridge University Press, 1996), pp. 234–327, here pp. 301, 302 (Ak. 7:84, 85).

founding of the UN and its human rights policy. I will attempt to assemble the various pieces of the puzzle into a constructive image of a global democratic order (III).

II The European Union must decide between transnational democracy and post-democratic executive federalism

The dense network of supranational organizations has long inspired fears that the connection between civil rights and democracy vouched for by the nation state could be destroyed and the democratic sovereigns disenfranchised by globally operating independent executive powers.[17] Two different issues combine to prompt this unease. Reasons of space prevent me from commenting on the legitimate empirical question of an economic dynamic within world society which has for decades been exacerbating a long-standing democratic deficit.[18] Taking the example of the European Union, I would like

---

[17] See the critique of Ingeborg Maus, 'Menschenrechte als Ermächtigungsnormen internationaler Politik oder: der zerstörte Zusammenhang von Menschenrechten und Demokratie', in Hauke Brunkhorst, Wolfgang R. Köhler and Matthias Lutz-Bachmann (eds), *Recht auf Menschenrechte: Menschenrechte, Demokratie und internationale Politik* (Frankfurt am Main: Suhrkamp, 1999), pp. 276–92; Maus, 'Verfassung oder Vertrag: Zur Verrechtlichung globaler Politik', in Peter Niesen and Benjamin Herborth (eds), *Anarchie der kommunikativen Freiheit; Jürgen Habermas und die Theorie der internationalen Politik* (Frankfurt am Main: Suhrkamp, 2007), pp. 350–82.

[18] Michael Zürn and Matthias Ecker-Ehrhardt (eds), *Die Politisierung der Weltpolitik* (forthcoming); see also David Held and Anthony McGrew (eds), *The Global Transformations Reader: An Introduction to the Globalization Debate* (Cambridge: Polity, 2000).

to address the other thesis on which the political defeatism of the Eurosceptics is primarily based – namely, the assertion that a transnationalization of popular sovereignty is impossible without lowering the level of legitimation.

For this purpose I must first remove a mental block which obstructs the view ahead by suggesting that popular sovereignty depends conceptually on state sovereignty (1). I will then proceed to conceptualize the transnationalization of popular sovereignty with the aid of three variable components which are exactly aligned only at the national level. The three components are, first, the democratic association of free and equal legal persons, second, the organization of collective decision-making powers and, finally, the medium of integration of civic solidarity among strangers. These components enter into a new configuration at the European level. The two remarkable innovations here are that the member states, who retain their monopoly on the legitimate use of force, subordinate themselves to supranational law, albeit with an interesting proviso (2), and that they share their 'sovereignty' in a certain sense with the citizenry of the Union as a whole (3). This reconfiguration of the components of a democratic community into the shape of a federation beyond the nation state does not imply a loss of legitimacy because the citizens of Europe have good reasons for wanting their respective nation states to *continue to perform their constitutional role* as guarantors of law and freedom. In that case, however, the 'sharing of sovereignty' between the citizens of the European Union and the peoples of Europe would also have to be transformed into a consistently implemented co-legislation and into the symmetrical accountability of the Commission to the Council and the Parliament (4). In conclusion, I will return to the theme of the limits of civic solidarity which are becoming apparent in the current crisis (5).

1 Against a reification of popular sovereignty

Before we can clarify the possibility of an uncoupling of the democratic procedure from the nation state, we first need to know how we want to understand democracy. Democratic self-government means that the addressees of mandatory laws are at the same time their authors. In a democracy, citizens are subject only to those laws which they have given themselves in accordance with a democratic procedure.[19] The legitimizing force of this procedure rests, on the one hand, on the inclusion of all citizens in the political decision-making processes (however this is realized) and, on the other, on the coupling of (if necessary qualified) majority decisions with deliberative will-formation. Such a model of democracy transforms the citizens' use of communicative freedoms into as many productive forces for the legitimate – i.e. both interest-aggregating and effective – *self-influencing of a politically organized civil society*. If the citizens are to be able to cooperate in influencing social conditions,

---

[19] On the democratic procedure and on the deliberative understanding of democratic politics in general, see my essays 'Three normative models of democracy', in *The Inclusion of the Other*, pp. 239–52, and 'Political communication in media society: does democracy still have an epistemic dimension? The impact of normative theory on empirical research', in *Europe: The Faltering Project*, trans. Ciaran Cronin (Cambridge: Polity, 2009), pp. 138–83.

then the state must have corresponding scope for the political shaping of living conditions. In this sense there is a conceptual connection between popular sovereignty and state sovereignty. In view of a politically unregulated growth in the complexity of world society which is placing increasingly narrow systemic restrictions on the scope for action of nation states, the requirement to extend political decision-making capabilities beyond national borders follows from the normative meaning of democracy itself. To be sure, the states have sought to compensate for the resulting loss in their problem-solving capacities with the help of international organizations;[20] but, quite apart from the problem of the power asymmetry in the composition of most international treaty regimes, the states involved, assuming they have democratic constitutions, pay the price of sinking levels of legitimacy for a form of governance founded on intergovernmentality. The fact that the governments who appoint their representatives to international organizations are democratically elected cannot offset this damage either.[21] Hence, the increase in power of international organizations actually undermines the democratic procedures in nation states to the extent that national functions shift to the level of transnational governance.

---

[20] On this, see Michael Zürn, 'Die Rückkehr der Demokratiefrage: Perspektiven demokratischen Regierens und die Rolle der Politikwissenschaft', *Blätter für deutsche und internationale Politik* 6 (2011): 63–74.

[21] On the reasons, see Christoph Möllers, *Die drei Gewalten: Legitimation der Gewaltengliederung in Vefassungsstaat, Europäischer Integration und Internationalisierung* (Weilerswist: Velbrück Wissenschaft, 2008), pp. 158ff.

If one does not want to resign oneself to this, while nevertheless having to acknowledge that the growing dependence of nation states on the systemic constraints of an increasingly interdependent world society is irreversible, then the political necessity of extending democratic procedures beyond national borders imposes itself. This necessity is a logical implication of the idea of a democratic civil society influencing its own conditions of existence: 'if a system is more democratic to the extent that it permits citizens to govern themselves on matters that are important to them, then in many circumstances a larger system would be more democratic than a smaller one, since its capacity to cope with certain matters – defence and pollution, for example – would be greater.'[22] Of course, this is not sufficient to dispel the doubt over whether the transnationalization of popular sovereignty is even possible.[23] It goes without saying that imperatives which follow from the logic of democracy itself under changed conditions can be thwarted by reality. The most stubborn scepticism concerning a *democratic* legal domestication of political authority that reaches beyond national borders, however, is nourished by a collectivist misunderstanding which confuses popular and state sovereignty. This misconception, which occurs in communitarian and liberal as well as in conservative and nationalistic readings, is based on an over-generalization of a contingent

---

[22] Robert A. Dahl, 'Federalism and the democratic process', in J. Roland Pennock and John W. Chapman (eds), *Nomos XXV: Liberal Democracy* (New York: New York University Press, 1983), pp. 95–108, here p. 105.

[23] Thomas Groß, 'Postnationale Demokratie: Gibt es ein Menschenrecht auf transnationale Selbstbestimmung?' *Rechtswissenschaft* 2 (2011): 125–53.

historical constellation and obscures the artificial, and thus floating, character of the consciousness of national identity constituted in nineteenth-century Europe.[24]

Citizens who participate in a democratic election and who authorize a few to act on behalf of all certainly engage in a *collective* practice. But this transforms democratically generated decisions into decisions of a collective only in a *distributively general* sense. For these decisions are the product of a plurality of individual stances which are generated and processed in accordance with democratic rules. Only a collectivistic reading makes results of pluralistic processes of opinion- and will-formation into expressions of a sovereign will of the people which authorizes itself to act. And only on the basis of this reifying singularization can popular sovereignty be presented *as the reverse side* of state sovereignty. It then appears to be the mirror image of the sovereignty of a state which, according to classical international law, is equipped with the *ius ad bellum* and as a consequence enjoys an unrestricted freedom of action – that is, one which is restricted only by the decisions of competing subjects of international law.[25] From such a perspective, the idea of popular sovereignty finds

[24] Hagen Schulze, *States, Nations, and Nationalism: From the Middle Ages to the Present*, trans. William E. Yuill (Oxford and New York: Blackwell, 1996), p. 175.

[25] Keeping in mind the empirical preconditions for the actual autonomy of action of a state whose borders are internationally recognized, and which as a result by no means operates in a legal vacuum, reveals the semantic surplus which has always been associated with – and, ironically, in spite of worldwide interdependence continues to be associated with – this concept (which originated in absolutism). On this, see, for the present context, Neil Walker (ed.), *Sovereignty in Transition* (Oxford: Hart, 2003).

17

its fulfilment in the external sovereignty of the state: in the actions of the state, the citizens can regard themselves in a certain sense as the jointly acting members of a political collectivity.[26]

Admittedly, republican freedom, universal conscription and nationalism all had the same historical origin in the French Revolution. However, the suggestive power of the figure of thought which establishes a *strong* connection between internal democratic self-government and external state sovereignty should not be generalized beyond this historical context. For the *freedom of action* of sovereign states guaranteed in classical international law is different from the *autonomy under the 'laws of freedom'* (Kant) which the citizens in constitutional states can make use of. Whereas the external sovereignty of the state is conceived in accordance with the model of freedom of choice, the sovereignty of the people is expressed in a democratically generalizing form of lawmaking which guarantees all citizens equal liberties. There is a fundamental conceptual difference between 'freedom of choice' and 'legal freedom'. For this reason, restricting national sovereignty by transferring sovereign rights to supranational authorities by no means *necessarily* comes at the cost of disenfranchising democratic citizens. Such a transfer, *if it only leaves the*

---

[26] Carl Schmitt, in *Constitutional Theory* (trans. and ed. Jeffrey Seitzer [Durham, NC: Duke University Press, 2008], § 17), inverted this relationship into the exaggerated reading of a plebiscitary 'Führerdemokratie': In exercising their collective self-assertion, especially in war, the national citizens existentially affirm a political constitution which, although it doesn't guarantee them any democratic participation, does allow them to take stances through plebiscites.

democratic procedure intact, carries forward precisely the kind of constitutionalization of political authority to which citizens within the nation state already owe their liberties.

Then the competences delegated to or shared with supranational authorities by the nation state may not be codified in law in international treaty regimes alone, however; they must be codified in law in a *democratic* manner. A transfer of sovereign rights does not diminish the scope of civic autonomy only on the condition that the citizens of the one affected state cooperate with the citizens of the other affected states in making supranational law *in accordance with a democratic procedure.*[27] An increase in territorial scale alone – i.e. a merely numerical enlargement of the basic population of participants – changes the complexity, but not necessarily the quality, of the process of opinion- and will-formation. This is why there can be no question of a restriction of popular sovereignty as long as quantitative changes in the social and spatial dimension leave the process itself intact – that is, as long as they do not impair deliberation and inclusion.[28]

---

[27] With this 'strong' condition I exclude all compromise proposals which reduce the legitimatory requirements on supranational decision-making processes. Democratic legitimation cannot be replaced by one of its moments (such as responsibility, deliberative justification, transparency or the rule of law). On this discussion, see the contributions by Jürgen Neyer, Erik Oddvar Erikson, Frank Nullmeier and Tanja Pritzlaff in Rainer Forst and Rainer Schmalz-Bruns (eds), *Political Legitimacy and Democracy in Transnational Perspective*, Arena Report no. 2/11, University of Oslo, 2011.

[28] Even a sceptic such as William E. Scheuerman does not attach any weight in principle to the supposed advantages of limited geographical scope in this regard. On this, see his essay 'Der Republikanismus der Aufklärung

Hence, it will be possible to democratize the international network that has emerged in the meantime only if it proves possible to assemble the components familiar from national democracies differently from in the nation state without a loss of legitimacy. In this regard, the test which the European Union currently has to undergo is instructive. For what is being tested is the will and capability of citizens, of political elites and the mass media, to conclude the next stage of integration at least within the euro zone – and in the process to take the civilization of the exercise of political authority a step further.

2 The first innovation: the primacy of supranational law over the national law of the monopolists on the means for a legitimate use of force

The European Union will be able to achieve long-term stability only if it takes the steps towards coordinating the relevant policies necessitated by the economic imperatives via a sufficiently democratic mode of juridification, rather than in the gubernatorial-bureaucratic style customary until now. However, we become entangled in the next constitutional political steps as long as

im Zeitalter der Globalisierung', in Oliver Eberl (ed.), *Transnationalisierung der Volkssouveränität*, pp. 251–70. There he writes: '*Kleinräumigkei*, in short, is not an historical *given* determining the proper extent of state territory in some immediately identifiable manner, but instead an historically alterable condition subject to the ongoing "compression of space and time"' (p. 265). On the other hand, we should not play down the danger of systematic distortion to which the circuits of communication are subject in geographically extensive and heterogeneous political public spheres – especially under conditions of (almost) completely privatized media, as in the United States.

we remain within the conceptual spectrum extending from a confederation of states (*Staatenbund*) to a federal state (*Bundesstaat*) or are content to negate this alternative in an *indeterminate manner*. Before we are able to grasp what the European decisions still lack in order to become legitimate, we must first acknowledge the democratic character of the form already assumed by the European Union as a result of the Treaty of Lisbon.[29]

To this end, I distinguish three building blocks[30] which must find embodiment in one way or another in every democratic political community:

- the process through which legal persons come together in a limited geographical space to form an association of free and equal citizens by granting each other rights which guarantee everyone equal private and civic autonomy;
- the distribution of powers within an organization which secures the collective decision-making power of the association of citizens by administrative means; and
- the medium of integration of civic solidarity within and across national borders which is a necessary condition for joint political will-formation and hence for both the communicative generation of democratic

---

[29] Ingolf Pernice, 'Verfassungsverbund', in Franzius, Mayer and Neyer (eds), *Strukturfragen der Europäischen Union*, pp. 102–9.

[30] Hauke Brunkhorst, 'A polity without a state? European constitutionalism between evolution and revolution', in Erik Oddvar Eriksen, John Erik Fossum and Augustin José Menéndez (eds), *Developing a Constitution for Europe* (London: Routledge, 2004); Brunkhorst, 'State and constitution: a reply to Scheuerman', *Constellations* 15 (2008): 493–501.

power and the legitimation of the exercise of political authority.[31]

From the perspective of the legal system, the first two components are usually addressed in the parts of the constitution dealing with fundamental rights and the organization of legal capacities, whereas the third component refers to the 'people' as the functional requirement for the democratic process – that is, in the first instance, to the political-cultural conditions for appropriate communication processes in the political public sphere. Because the constitution connects law and politics through the legal medium, the following distinction is important for differentiating between the perspectives of legal and political science. Only the associational component has an *immediate* legal character because civil society is *first constituted* in the medium of the law; a political community which satisfies the conditions of democratic legitimacy must assume the form of a horizontally integrated association of legal consociates. The second component, comprising the institutions and organization of the state, regulates access to politi-

---

[31] The three components are building blocks of a political system. They relate to

- the constitution of a community of legal persons;
- the authorization to collective action; and
- the shared horizon of a lifeworld in which a collective will can take shape through communication.

This does not, however, imply a bias in favour of an exclusively action-theoretical analysis in political science. The political public sphere communicates about the organization of the state with all other *functional systems* of society in the language of the law which circulates throughout society.

cal power – here the flows of administrative power are legally channelled (whereby the administrative system interacts with other functional systems of society); the third component, which relates to the political-cultural background functionally necessary for opinion- and will-formation, can only be presupposed by law and can at best be promoted through political measures.

These three components come together in a *congruent* fashion only at the national level, be it in the form of a unitary or of a federal state. In such a constitutional state, governmental authority is programmed through the democratic process and in the grammar of general laws in such a way that the citizens can exercise their authority through legislative, executive and judicial bodies. The citizens of a democratic political community do not subject themselves to the law simply as a matter of fact because of the threat of sanctions by the state; they can also accept the law in principle as 'right' because it was enacted through a democratic procedure. This way of bringing the exercise of political authority under the sway of democratic legislation amounts to *civilizing violence* insofar as the executive elected by the people, even though it disposes over the means for a legitimate use of force, must follow the law. This 'must' does not express a factual constraint, but a politically and culturally established normative 'ought'. Every military coup of the kind familiar from façade democracies and every coup supported by economically powerful or socially influential elites shows that this is by no means self-evident.

Already at the national level, therefore, the civilizing element consists in subordinating arbitrary violence to the law legitimately enacted by (and in the name of) those who are subjected to political authority. Needless to say, it belongs to the meaning of the validity of positive law that deviant behaviour incurs public sanctions. But who sanctions the monopolist on the legitimate use of force when it wants to do something else? Already within the nation state, the monopolists on the legitimate use of force who ensure compliance with the laws are subordinate to democratic law. But whereas here the institutions which make and enforce law are bodies of *the same* state, in the European Union law is made and enforced at different levels. At first sight, the arrangement seems to be similar to the one in federal states. Federal law also trumps state law in the multilevel system of the Federal Republic of Germany, even though the governments of the states (or *Länder*) retain control over the police (though not over the federal army). Nevertheless there is a decisive difference between the national and the European multilevel system.

Whereas in federally organized nation states the authority to change the constitution generally remains the privilege of the federation, in the European Union a priority of European law over the law of the member states has become firmly established, even though the organs of the Union do not possess such an authority.[32] Even if the member states can no longer regard themselves implicitly as 'sovereign subjects of the treaties', they have to give their unanimous consent to any regular revision of the treaty. Therefore the supranational

---

[32] Christian Calliess, *Die neue Europäische Union nach dem Vertrag von Lissabon: Ein Überblick über die Reformen unter Berücksichtigung ihrer Implikationen für das deutsche Recht* (Tübingen: Mohr Siebeck, 2010), pp. 84f. and 352ff.

political community constitutes itself as a legal community and preserves the binding character of European Union law even without the backing of the monopoly on the legitimate use of force and final decision-making authority. With this arrangement, the balance in the relation between the sanctioning power of the state and the law shifts. In exercising its legislative and judicial competences, the European Union binds the member states as the bodies which must implement its decisions even though it does not dispose over their sanctioning powers. And the national monopolists over the legitimate use of force allow themselves to be enlisted for the application of European law which has to be 'implemented' at the national level. With this first of the two innovations, which I regard as important steps towards the legal domestication of the violence at the core of the state, the constitution of the supranational political community sets itself apart from the national organizational institutions of its members.

But how should the priority of European law be understood? The decisions of the European Court of Justice since the 1963 Van Gend en Loos decision were groundbreaking. Since then, the Court has repeatedly stressed that the concrete willingness of the member states to comply is essential for the equal legal treatment of the citizens of the Union.[33] These decisions merely draw the logical conclusion from the fact that the European treaties have established a direct legal relation between the institutions and the citizens of

---

[33] Claudio Franzius, *Europäisches Verfassungsrechtsdenken* (Tübingen: Mohr Siebeck, 2010), pp. 38ff.

the Union, and have thereby created an autonomous level of law independent from the law of the member states. On the other hand, the lack of the authority to amend the constitution (or, in the terminology of the nineteenth century, the competence to decide about its own competence (*Kompetenz-Kompetenz*)) unavoidably affects how the status of the national vis-à-vis the new European legal level is conceptualized. If the Union is not authorized to make final decisions, the subordination of national law under European Union law actually in effect cannot be explained in terms of the customary hierarchical relation between federal and state law or between constitutional law and secondary law. The priority of European law conforms to a different logic. Claudio Franzius speaks of a functionally justified 'primacy of application'[34] and Armin von Bogdandy of the 'efficacy' of European law which 'obliges the member states to realize the regulatory purpose of a norm of Community law'.[35]

But how can a 'primacy of application' be grounded in the autonomy of Community law if this level of law cannot claim a 'primacy of validity' over the national legal systems? Even the Federal Constitutional Court in Karlsruhe, in its decisions on the Maastricht and Lisbon treaties, insists only on a *reservation* of the national constitutions vis-à-vis European legislation. Notwithstanding the justified criticism of these two far from Europe-friendly rulings, the national courts,

---

[34] Ibid., p. 42.
[35] Armin von Bogdandy, 'Grundprinzipien', in von Bogdandy and Bast (eds), *Europäisches Verfassungsrecht*, pp. 13–71, here p. 38.

in their interpretations of the European treaties, can conceive of themselves as legitimate guardians of the democratic legal substance of the constitutions of their respective member countries. The national courts are not authorized (as the Federal Constitutional Court incorrectly assumes)[36] to monitor the limits of the transfer of national sovereign rights to the European level, though they are authorized (as entailed by TEU, Art. 4, para. 2) to safeguard the inviolability of those national constitutional principles which are constitutive for democracy and the rule of law in the respective member states. The conflicts between the courts at the two levels[37] reflect a complementary dependence and interconnection between national constitutions and Community law which has inspired Ingolf Pernice to describe the Union as a 'constitutional alliance'.[38] In order to explain why the member states, which continue to exercise a monopoly over the means for a legitimate use of force, subordinate themselves to the law of the Community, even though the latter cannot claim any higher authority to amend the constitution, we must anticipate the second of the two constitutional legal innovations mentioned above. From the perspective of

[36] Christoph Schönberger, 'Lisbon in Karlsruhe: Maastricht's epigones at sea', *German Law Journal* 10 (2009): 1201–18; Daniel Halberstam and Christoph Möllers, 'The German constitutional court says Ja zu Deutschland!', *German Law Journal* 10 (2009): 1241–58.

[37] The Spanish constitutional court would like to resolve these conflicts semantically by means of the concepts *premacía* and *supremacía*; see Claudio Franzius, *Europäisches Verfassungsrechtsdenken*, p. 47.

[38] Ingolf Pernice, 'Europäisches und nationales Verfassungsrecht', *Veröffentlichungen der Vereinigung der Deutschen Staatsrechtslehrer* 60 (2001): 149–93.

a *rationally reconstructed* constitution-building process, the subordination under European law can be understood as a result of the fact that, from the very beginning, two different subjects were involved who cooperated in bringing about a supranational political community.

With regard to a constitutionalization of international law, I note first that, with the European Union, a politically constituted community has emerged which enjoys binding legislative authority in relation to its member states without the backing of congruent state powers. At the beginning of the process of European unification, the chief expression of the civilizing power of this innovation was the pacification of a continent drenched in blood; in the meantime this power manifests itself in the struggle to construct high-level political decision-making capabilities. In this way, the peoples of a continent whose political and economic weight is diminishing are trying to recover a certain political room for manoeuvre in the face of the political forces and systemic restraints of a globalized society. If they succeed, they can use this room for manoeuvre not only defensively to preserve their cultural biotope but also offensively for a further and still more toilsome construction of global steering capacities. I will return to this below.

3 The second innovation: the sharing of constituting power between EU citizens and European peoples

When the constitutional community of European citizens detaches itself from the organizational cores of the member states,[39] all three components of a constitution enter into a new constellation. Whereas the member states retain their monopoly over the means for a legitimate use of force and transfer sovereign rights to the Union through a limited conferral of powers, the Union can rely only on a relatively weak organizational component. Contrary to the popular image of the 'Brussels monster',[40] the European Commission is composed of a relatively limited bureaucracy which leaves the 'implementation' of European Union law to the parliaments and administrations of the member states.[41] And because the Union does not acquire a state-like character, the citizens of the Union do not enjoy the status of *state* citizens in the strict sense either. There is nevertheless the expectation that the growing mutual trust among the European peoples will give rise to a transnational, though attenuated, form of civic solidarity among the citizens of the Union.

With the exacting requirement that these same persons must learn to distinguish between the role of a member of a 'European people' and that of a 'citizen of the Union', we touch on the central question of the correct constitutional concept for this new kind of federal polity. The negative information that the Union can be defined neither as a confederation of states nor

---

[39] Christian Calliess speaks in terms of a 'material understanding of the constitution which separates the concept of the constitution from the state' (*Die neue Europäische Union*, p. 73).

[40] Hans Magnus Enzensberger, *Sanftes Monster Brüssel oder Die Entmündigung Europas* (Berlin: Suhrkamp, 2011).

[41] On the welcome role of the national parliaments as the custodians of subsidiarity, see Calliess, *Die neue Europäische Union*, pp. 182ff.

as a federal state is not sufficient as an answer. The prominent status that the Treaty of Lisbon accords the European Council and the Council of Ministers reflects the historical role of the member states as the initiators and driving forces of European unification. In contrast to various national constitutions in the eighteenth and nineteenth centuries, the constitution of the Union is the work of political elites. Whereas revolutionary citizens once united to overthrow old regimes, on this occasion it was states, i.e. collective actors, that used the instrument of international treaties to join forces in order to cooperate in limited areas of policy. In spite of this active role played by the states, however, over the course of the unification process the balance has shifted dramatically within the organizational structure in favour of the European citizens.[42]

The international organization has been transformed into a political Union of indefinite duration. With the introduction of citizenship of the Union, with the explicit reference to a common European weal and with the recognition of the Union as an autonomous legal personality, the treaties have become the foundation of a political community with a constitution of its own. Admittedly, the term 'constitutional treaty', by contrast with the democratic constitution of a national federal state, may point to the peculiarity that the European Union wants to be understood as a *supranational*, though nevertheless democratically constituted

---

[42] On this, see Jürgen Bast, 'Europäische Gesetzgebung: Fünf Stationen in der Verfassungsentwicklung der EU', in Franzius, Mayer and Neyer (eds), *Strukturfragen der Europäischen Union*, pp. 173–80.

(and correspondingly legitimized), political community. The Union shares this supranational character with the federations of the pre-democratic era, the ancient empires and alliances of city states; but, in contrast to the classical state alliances, the structure of the Union is supposed to conform unequivocally to democratic principles. In declamatory terms, Articles 9 to 12 of the Lisbon Treaty leave nothing to be desired in this regard.[43]

A suitable way of clarifying the constitutional and legal structure of this peculiar formation is to reconstruct its history of emergence, interpreted in teleological terms, as though the more or less contingent historical outcome had been the deliberate result of a regular constitutional convention. When we look for an equivalent for the role played between September 1787 and August 1788 in the North American case by the letters, essays and speeches of the federalists and antifederalists,[44] in Europe we come across scarcely a single committed public debate among educated laypersons and intellectuals.[45] Here the field was dominated for decades by a discussion among

---

[43] On this, see the emphatic account in Armin von Bogdandy, *Democratic Legitimacy of Public Authority beyond the State – Lessons from the EU for International Organizations*, working paper (April 2011), available online: http://ssrn.com/abstract=1826326 (accessed September 2011).

[44] Bernard Baylin, *The Debate on the Constitution: Federalist and Antifederalist Speeches, Articles, and Letters during the Struggle over Ratification, September 1787–August 1788*, 2 vols (New York: Library of America, 1993).

[45] On the national contexts of the highly fragmented discussion among European intellectuals, see Justine Lacroix and Kalypso Nicolaïdis (eds), *European Stories: Intellectual Debates on Europe in National Contexts* (Oxford: Oxford University Press, 2010).

highly specialized experts, especially lawyers but also political and social scientists.[46] To be fair, it must be noted that 'much of the best scholarly imagination has flowed into efforts to develop the European Union in a democratic way and public opinion has participated in these efforts.'[47]

Just as in North America at that time, a controversy has also broken out among us between the Eurosceptic champions of the states and the federalists over the transfer of sovereignty rights to the Union. In contrast to the American immigrant societies in the colonial states striving for independence, however, the European federalists encounter the linguistic and cultural diversity, and above all the political stubbornness, of the *first generation* of evolved and war-hardened nation states (which also differ from each other with regard to the construction of their social welfare systems during the twentieth century). Moreover, the European unification, unlike the American, does not find itself at the beginning of experimentation with forms of federation under conditions of the modern system of states. Today all federations have adapted themselves more or less to the nation state model; the United States, too, has become a federal state at the latest since the end of the Second World War. The United Nations can understand itself at the beginning of the twenty-first century as an

---

[46] A good survey of the debates over Europe in Great Britain, France and Germany is provided by Richard Münch, *Die Konstruktion der Europäischen Gesellschaft: Zur Dialektik von transnationaler Integration und nationaler Desintegration* (Frankfurt am Main: Campus, 2008), pp. 186–340.

[47] Armin von Bogdandy, verbal communication.

association of 193 nation states.[48] The question that James Madison already confronted in 1787 arises all the more urgently with regard to the European Union: can a federation of member states with democratic constitutions satisfy the conditions of democratic legitimation without clearly subordinating the national level to the federal level?[49]

Madison consistently linked the question of legitimacy with that of the constitution of the Union. His answer was that the ensemble of founding states had to agree unanimously on a merger, while the constitution had to connect and balance the competences between the two political levels in such a way that possible conflicts between the constitutional organs could be resolved pragmatically without a clear priority rule. By eschewing a normative commitment in the question of who should have the final say, he also left open who exactly could be meant by the subject of the first sentence of the text of the constitution, 'We the People of the United States' – the citizenry of the union as a whole or the peoples of the separate states. As Madison conceived it, it was a matter for politics to strike the appropriate balance in cases of conflict. Contemporary authors who take their orientation from these conceptions[50] admittedly garner good arguments from them

---

[48] Carl Schmitt duly regards the federal state as the 'the resolution of the antinomies of the federation' (*Constitutional Theory*, p. 392).

[49] Bernard Baylin, *The Debate on the Constitution*, Vol. 2: *January to August 1788*, pp. 26–32.

[50] Robert Schütze, 'On "federal" ground: the European Union as an (inter) national phenomenon', *Common Market Law Review* 46 (2009): 1069–105.

against narrowing down the discussion over Europe to the alternative between a confederation of states and the federal state familiar from German constitutional history.[51] However, the customary recourse to Carl Schmitt's 'constitutional theory of federation' in this context evades the issue of the democratic legitimation of the federation,[52] because Schmitt suppresses the normative question concerning the bearer of the constituent power 'of the people'. In contrast to Madison, he has in mind the pre-democratic forms of federation and confines himself to the political decision-making process within the constituted federation.

A satisfactory answer can be found to the question of legitimation which interests us only if we identify the constitution-founding powers correctly. After Article 1, paragraph 2, of the 1992 Treaty of Maastricht had given the starting signal for an 'ever closer union among the *peoples* of Europe', Article 1, paragraph 1, of the Treaty Establishing a Constitution for Europe already referred to both subjects – both the 'citizens' and 'the States' of Europe.[53] Even though this constitution drawn up by a convention in 2004 was never adopted, the Lisbon Treaty currently in effect supports

---

[51] Oeter, 'Föderalismus und Demokratie'; see also the critique of the federal state premises of the Federal Constitutional Court in Karlsruhe presented by Christoph Schönberger in his essay 'Lisbon in Karlsruhe: Maastricht's epigones at sea'.

[52] Christoph Schönberger, 'Die Europäische Union als Bund', *Archiv des öffentlichen Rechts* 129 (2004): 81–120.

[53] 'Reflecting the will of the citizens and States of Europe to build a common future, this Constitution establishes the European Union, on which the Member States confer competences to attain objectives they have in common.'

the thesis that sovereignty is 'shared' between the citizens and the states[54] for the simple reason that the Parliament is involved (albeit to a limited extent) when the Constitutional Treaty is amended, and it is a body on a par with the Council of Ministers within the 'ordinary legislative procedure'.

However, an important qualification must be made from the perspective of democratic theory to the splitting of the constituent subject into 'citizens' and 'states'.[55] Citizens are involved in a twofold manner in constituting the higher-level political community – directly in their role as future EU citizens and indirectly in their role as members of one of the national peoples. This is why the EU constitution, like all modern legal systems, has a strictly individualistic character, in spite of the fact that one of the two supporting pillars is composed *directly* of collectivities. It rests *in the final analysis* on the subjective rights of the citizens. It is therefore more consistent to recognize not the member states themselves but their peoples as the other constitution-founding subject. 'Once the question of the principle of democracy arises, the treaties speak on the one hand of the peoples of the member states and on the other of the citizens of the Union.'[56]

---

[54] Calliess, *Die neue Europäische Union nach dem Vertrag von Lissabon*, p. 71.

[55] I am grateful to Peter Niesen for this important reference.

[56] Von Bogdandy, 'Grundprinzipien', p. 64. The reference to Kant is interesting in this context; on this, see the commentary of Oliver Eberl and Peter Niesen on Kant's *Zum ewigen Frieden* (Berlin: Suhrkamp, 2011), p. 166: 'Kant speaks of the freedom of peoples, however, not of states . . . This indicates that Kant is concerned . . . with the constitutional and legal freedom of peoples and not with the freedom of states as understood in international law.'

Following Anne Peters, Claudio Franzius also argues for the assumption of a *pouvoir constituant mixte.*[57] If we conceive of the individual citizens as the only source of legitimation in this way, we must avoid setting the wrong course. The issue is whether we recognize in these constitution-founding subjects 'originally' the citizens of the founding states who first empower themselves as EU citizens through the constitution-building process, as James Madison thought,[58] or whether in them we encounter the future EU citizens *directly.* The choice between these unhappy alternatives would in turn create a precedent in favour of ascribing final decision-making authority to either the Union or its members. The more consistent approach to solving the problem of the yardstick against which the democratic character of a federative political community beyond the nation state is measured is suggested by Armin von Bogdandy: 'Theoretically speaking it is more convincing to conceive of the individuals, *who are (simultaneously) citizens of the states and of the Union,* as the only subject of legitimation.'[59]

On our scenario, it is *the same* persons who participate in the constitution-building process simultaneously

---

[57] Claudio Franzius writes on this: 'The citizens sustain the constitution-alization process as national citizens and as EU citizens' (*Europäisches Verfassungsrechtsdenken,* p. 57).

[58] In this sense, Ingolf Pernice defends the view that sovereign rights are transferred to the European Union 'originally by the citizens of the member states jointly' ('Verfassungsverbund', p. 106). From this he draws the conclusion that 'EU citizenship is the shared political status referring to the Union and its legitimation which the citizens of the member states as national citizens have conferred upon themselves through the European Union constitution' (ibid., p. 108).

[59] Von Bogdandy, 'Grundprinzipien', p. 64 (my parenthetical addition, JH).

in the roles of (future) citizens of both the Union and the member states. In exercising these two roles in personal union, the constitution-funding subjects themselves must become aware that, as citizens, they will adopt a different justice perspective depending on which of the two legitimation tracks running through the Parliament and the Council, respectively, is involved – namely, the perspective of a European citizen or that of a member of a particular nation. What counts as a public interest orientation within a particular nation state changes at the European level into a particularistic generalization of interests confined to one's own people which may well come into conflict with the Europe-wide generalization of interests expected from EU citizens. In this way, the two role aspects of the constitution-founding subjects acquire an institutional meaning for the constituted political community: at the European level, the citizens should be able to form judgements and make political decisions simultaneously and on an equal footing as EU citizens and as members of a particular nation belonging to the EU. Every citizen participates in the European opinion- and will-formation processes both as an *individual* European who autonomously says 'yes' and 'no' and as a *member* of a particular nation.

4 Shared sovereignty as the standard for the legitimation requirements of the Union

The expression 'shared sovereignty' is ambiguous.[60] The sovereignty of the people – i.e. the 'power' which is

---

[60] Note that the German term 'geteilte Souveränität' can mean either 'shared sovereignty' or 'divided sovereignty' (*Trans.*).

'derived from the people' – branches and spreads within every democratically constituted political community from the beginning into the flows of communication within the legislature, the executive and the judiciary. But a different and peculiar kind of 'shared' sovereignty is involved in the present case. The division of the constituent power divides sovereignty *at the origin of a political community which is going to be constituted*, and not only *at the source of the already constituted political community*. This division explains why the European Union shares with federal states the character of a multilevel system; but the EU must not be understood as a kind of *imperfect* federal republic. Even nation states which have an internal federal structure are also constituted by the entire national citizenry alone.[61] By contrast, the foundation of the European Union can be conceived retrospectively as though the citizens involved (or their representatives) were split into two *personae* from the beginning; in that case every person as a European citizen in the constitution-founding process encounters herself, as it were, as a citizen of an already constituted national people.

In federal states, the distribution of powers can

---

[61] It is a surprising fact that, as recently as 1995, some Supreme Court justices in the United States still insisted on interpreting the subject 'We the People', cited in Article 1, paragraph 1, of the United States Constitution (notwithstanding the grammatical singular), as referring to the aggregate of 'peoples' of the component states and not to the federal people. Nevertheless, although this is indeed a testimony to the stubbornness of old loyalties, it is not an argument against the conceptual necessity of differentiating between the level at which a political community is constituted and the levels constituted within it; on this case, see Schönberger, 'Die Europäische Union als Bund', pp. 81ff.

generally also be traced back to a limited case-by-case authorization of the federal organs by the member states. But as long as the citizens of a national state act as the sole constituent subject of that state, they not only lay down the primacy of federal law but also reserve the responsibility for making constitutional changes either for themselves (through national referenda) or for the federal legislative organs.[62] The conception of 'originally shared' popular sovereignty I am advancing precludes the possibility of such a supreme constitutional authority (*Kompetenz-Kompetenz*) at the European level. The constituent subjects are willing in their role as members of the (future) member states to transfer the sovereign rights of their already constituted states in part, and only one by one, to the new polity. Nevertheless, they do so with a reservation that goes far beyond the guarantee of the continued existence of the component states familiar from the constitutions of federal states. Instead, through their participation in the founding process, the European peoples ensure that their respective states survive within the federal polity *in their freedom-guaranteeing function* of constitutional states.

The constitutional political perspective that the Union *must not fall below* the level of taming and civilizing state power already achieved in the states also explains the reservation of the national constitutional

---

[62] This also holds for the Swiss Federal Constitution of 1999, even though, according to the Preamble and Article 1, paragraph 1, the Swiss Confederation is founded simultaneously by the 'Swiss People and the Cantons'. The organs of the federation actually enjoy the prerogatives (Art. 184–6) characteristic of the supreme constitutional authority of a federal state.

courts vis-à-vis the primacy of application of European law. The level of publicly guaranteed civil liberties at the national level should serve as a standard which European law must satisfy before it can be applied at the national level. This first renders intelligible the relatively strong status accorded the member states, which is reflected not only in the reservation of the monopoly on the legitimate use of force and in the (for the time being still disproportional) access to European legislation. There are two further interesting deviations from the federal state model.

Whereas Article V of the American constitution makes amendments contingent on the agreement of the legislative bodies of a qualified *majority* of the states,[63] amendments to the European treaties require (in accordance with the regular revision procedure specified in TEU, Art. 48) *unanimity* among the member states. The sovereignty of the member states *partially* preserved in the guarantee of a right of exit is given a similarly exemplary expression (TEU, Art. 50); although the Union was not founded for a definite duration, every member state is free to *regain* the degree of sovereignty it enjoyed before joining the Union. However, the modalities which must be taken into account before the decision to leave comes into effect show that the right of exit is not founded on 'a supreme constitutional authority

---

[63] Contrary to misleading comparisons between the European constitutional development and that in America, it must be pointed out that, with this definition, the US Constitution (in contrast to the European treaties) established the preconditions for a development over the course of which the United States has acquired the character of a constitutional state.

beholden to no other law than its own free choice';[64] for the original 'sharing of sovereignty' that a member state accepts when it joins the Union cannot be reconciled with the proviso that member states can make sovereign choices of their own.

The question arises, however, whether these deviations from the familiar pattern of legitimation do not ultimately reflect a deficit when measured against the standards of a *democratic* juridification of governance beyond the nation state. In my opinion, they need not represent a loss of legitimacy if the two constituent subjects – namely, the EU citizens and the European peoples – one day act consistently as equal partners in all legislative functions. As I said, the sharing of sovereignty as such can be justified by the fact that EU citizens have good reasons for insisting that their states should continue to play an equal role at the European level. As democratic states characterized by the rule of law, the nation states are not only actors on the long historical path towards civilizing the violence at the core of political power; as vital embodiments of 'existent justice' (Hegel), they also represent *lasting* achievements. Therefore, the citizens of the Union have a justified interest in their respective nation states *continuing* to perform their proven role as *guarantors of law and freedom* also in their role as member states. The nation states are more than just embodiments of national cultures worthy of preservation; they *vouch* for a level of justice and freedom which citizens rightly want to see preserved.

[64] Franzius, *Europäisches Verfassungsrechtsdenken*, p. 134; see also Schönberger, 'Die Europäische Union als Bund', p. 103.

At this point, the argument should not veer off in a communitarian direction. The interest in preserving *culturally* influential ways of living, in which the citizens recognize a part of their collective identity, is certainly *also* a constitutionally relevant reason. If this represented the decisive interest of citizens in preserving nation states, however, then it could be satisfied within the framework of a European federation through the principle of subsidiarity. Within a federation, the autonomy of the federated states or countries is recognized for the sake of protecting their historically shaped *socio-cultural and regional distinctiveness* – and not because these autonomous entities are still needed as *guarantors of the equal freedom of the citizens.*[65] It was precisely on account of this guarantee, however, that the members of the European peoples only wanted to *share* the constituent power with the EU citizens instead of being *subsumed by* the role of EU citizens – who in that case would also have acquired the exclusive authority to amend the constitution.

'Originally shared' sovereignty provides a standard for the legitimation requirements of a political commonwealth beyond the nation state. One can in this way not only justify the deviations from the model of a federal state but also identify the democratic deficits of the EU

---

[65] Of course, it is a political question, and, historically speaking, always a contingent result of social and political struggles, which constitutional definition is implemented for which identity-relevant frame of reference. See Christoph Möllers, 'Demokratische Ebenengliederung', in Ivo Appel, Georg Hermes and Christoph Schönberger (eds), *Öffentliches Recht im offenen Staat: Festschrift für Rainer Wahl* (Berlin: Duncker & Humblot, 2011), pp. 759–78.

treaties currently in force. Of course, the transnationalization of the elections to the European Parliament calls in the first place for a corresponding unified electoral law and, in addition, a certain Europeanization of the existing party system.[66] The main challenge at the institutional level, however, is to recover the equal standing and symmetric relation in the distribution of functions and legislative competences which we ascribe reconstructively to the European peoples and EU citizens as constitution-founding subjects. A balance between the competences of the Council and the Parliament must be achieved in all fields of policy. Also inconsistent is the peculiar floating position of the Commission, for which certain essential rights of initiative are reserved. Instead, the Commission, in a departure from the model of a federal government, should be equally dependent on the Parliament and the Council and be answerable to both institutions. The European Council, which is second in the list of organs after the Parliament in the Lisbon Treaty, is a complete anomaly.[67] As the seat of the intergovernmental political authority of the heads of government, it is – even more so than the Council of Ministers – the real counterweight to the Parliament, whereas its relationship to the Commission, which is supposed to see itself as the custodian of the interests of the Community, remains unclear.

---

[66] On this, see the study prepared by Claudio Franzius and Ulrich K. Preuß for the Heinrich Böll Foundation on 'Solidarität und Selbstbehauptung: Die Zukunft der EU im 21. Jahrhundert' [Solidarity and self-assertion: the future of the EU in the twenty-first century], unpublished MS, 2011.

[67] Calliess, *Die neue Europäische Union nach dem Vertrag von Lissabon*, pp. 118–28.

The European Council is a governing body which lays down policy guidelines, but it is authorized neither to pass legislation nor to issue directives to the Commission. Moreover, there is a strange contrast between the political power concentrated in the European Council and the fact that its decisions lack legal force. However, in virtue of its competence in the simplified treaty amendment procedure, it can spur innovations at the institutional level. Equipped with the strong legitimation of elected heads of government, it exercises considerable extra-constitutional power, even though it must reach decisions through consensus: 'As a political governing body, it is comparable to the king in the early constitutionalism of the nineteenth century.'[68] The Lisbon Treaty was supposed to confer enhanced decision-making power on the EU by incorporating the European Council into its institutional structure; but it pays a high price for this in the form of the lack of legitimacy of decisions with far-reaching implications. This is apparent since the 2008 financial crisis in the momentous decisions on guarantees for over-indebted states and on new modalities of extra-contractual harmonization of national budgets among the seventeen governments of the monetary union.

*5 The hesitation of the political elites at the threshold
to transnational democracy*
This observation calls to mind the complex *relation between treaty norm and treaty reality*. Empirical studies

---

[68] Franzius, *Europäisches Verfassungsrechtsdenken*, p. 58; similarly, von Bogdandy, 'Grundprinzipien', p. 44.

in political science which establish more or less drastic deviations of the actual circulation of power from the normatively required pattern often have an unmasking effect. Conjectures concerning superstructures are misplaced, however. It is not as though political practices are merely a dependent variable in the field of social interests, informal power relations and functional systemic constraints. Instead they obey a stubborn political code which is connected with the legal normative framework. This explains why innovative constitutional norms linking law and politics at the supranational level in many cases have a constructive anticipatory, stimulating effect by prompting learning and adaptation processes. This is why we adopt a constructivist perspective when we want to conceptualize the democratic legal domestication of a supranational political community such as the EU as a further stage in civilizing state power.[69]

The same perspective is also recommendable for social scientific analysis of the exacting political-cultural conditions which must be satisfied if transnational will-formation by citizens of the EU is to take place.[70] Until now we have addressed just two of the three components of democratic constitutions which enter into a new constellation at the European level. Once a constitutional community reaches beyond the boundaries of a single state, however, the third component – i.e.

---

[69] On social constructivism in international politics, see Bernhard Zangl and Michael Zürn, *Frieden und Krieg: Sicherheit in der nationalen und postnationalen Konstellation* (Frankfurt am Main: Suhrkamp, 2003), pp. 118–48.

[70] An interesting research approach is developed by Richard Münch (*Die Konstruktion der Europäischen Gesellschaft*, pp. 68ff.).

solidarity among citizens who are willing to support each other – should expand to keep pace with it, as it were. The EU citizenry as a whole can share sovereignty effectively with the peoples of the member states, which continue to enjoy a monopoly on the means for a legitimate use of force, only if national civic solidarity also undergoes a transformation. According to the scenario I propose, an extended, though also more abstract and hence comparatively less resilient, civic solidarity would have to include the members of each of the other European peoples – from the German perspective, for example, the Greeks when they are subjected to internationally imposed and socially unbalanced austerity programmes. Only in that case would the EU citizens who elect and control the Parliament in Strasbourg be able to participate in a joint process of democratic will-formation reaching across national borders.[71]

To be sure, the expansion of communication networks and horizons of perception, the liberalization of values and attitudes, an increase in the willingness to include strangers, the strengthening of civil society initiatives and a corresponding transformation of strong identities can at best be stimulated through legal-administrative means. There nevertheless exists a circular, either mutually reinforcing or mutually inhibiting, interaction between political processes and constitutional norms, on the one hand, and the network of shared political and cultural attitudes and convictions, on the other. This is how I understand Christoph

---

[71] Habermas, 'Is the development of a European identity necessary, and is it possible?', in *The Divided West*, pp. 67–82.

Möllers, who observes a 'co-evolution of democratic subjects of legitimation and democratic-egalitarian institutional arrangements'; this makes it possible 'to endow levels beyond the democratic state with further competences to act'.[72] When it comes to the constitutional definition of the boundaries of a political community and its subpopulations or to defining the tiers in a multilevel political system, there are no 'givens'; loyalties evolve and traditions change. Nations, too, just like all other comparable referents, are not natural facts, even if they are generally not merely fictions either (as was the case with many colonial state creations).

Many loyalties overlap in the political life of a citizen, loyalties to which individuals attach quite different weights. Among them are politically relevant ties with one's region of origin, with the state or province of one's domicile, with country or nation, etc. Only in cases of conflict do the weights attached to these loyalties acquire relevance because they have to be balanced against each other. A measure of the strength of an identification with one social unit rather than another is the willingness to make sacrifices based on longer-term relations of reciprocity. With the abolition of universal conscription, the test case of war, and hence the *absolute* claim to sacrifice one's life for the well-being of the nation, has fortunately lost its relevance. But the long shadow cast by nationalism continues to obscure the present. The supranational expansion of civic solidarity depends on learning processes which, as the current

---

[72] Möllers, 'Demokratische Ebenengliederung', pp. 775ff.

crisis leads us to hope, can be stimulated by perceptions of economic and political constraints.

In the meantime, the cunning of economic reason has at least set cross-border communication in train. The European institutions have long since staked out for the enfranchised EU citizens, with their wine-red passports, the virtual space which would have to be filled with life by appropriately extended communication processes within civil society. But this can take on concrete form only as the national public spheres gradually *open themselves up to each other*. The transnationalization of the existing national publics does not call for different news media, but instead for a different practice on the part of the existing leading media. Not only must the latter thematize and address European issues as such, but they must at the same time report on the political positions and controversies which the same topics evoke in other member states. A dangerous asymmetry has developed because until now the European Union has been sustained and monopolized by political elites – an asymmetry between the democratic participation of the *peoples* in what their governments 'obtain' for them on the, as they see it, far-off Brussels stage and the indifference, even apathy, of the *EU citizens* regarding the decisions of their parliament in Strasbourg.

However, this observation does not justify substantializing 'the people' or 'the nation'. The caricature of national macrosubjects shutting themselves off from each other and blocking any cross-border democratic will-formation is now the preserve of right-wing populism. After half a century of labour immigration, even the European peoples, given their growing ethnic, linguistic and religious diversity, can no longer be conceived as culturally homogenous entities.[73] In addition, the Internet and mass tourism have rendered national borders porous. Within the vast territories of our nation states, the floating horizon of a shared political lifeworld spanning large distances and complex relations *always* had to be produced and maintained by mass media, and it had to be lent substance by the abstract flows of ideas circulating through the communication networks of civil society. Such a process can acquire a secure foothold only on the basis of a shared political culture, however fluid it may be. But the more the national populations realize, *and the media help them to realize*, how profoundly the decisions of the European Union pervade their daily lives, the more their interest in making use of their democratic rights also as EU citizens will increase.

The impact factor of the perceived importance of European decisions has become palpable during the euro crisis. A reluctant European Council is being forced to make decisions that have patently unequal impacts on the budgets of the member states. As of 9 May 2009, the European Council has passed a threshold with its decisions on rescue packages and possible debt restructurings and its declarations of intent to bring about harmonization of the national budgets in all fields of relevance for competition – namely, economic, fiscal, labour market and social policy. Once this threshold is

---

[73] Klaus Eder, 'Europäische Öffentlichkeit und multiple Identitäten – das Ende des Volksbegriffs?', in Claudio Franzius and Ulrich K. Preuß (eds), *Europäische Öffentlichkeit* (Baden-Baden: Nomos, 2004), pp. 61–80.

crossed, new problems of distributive justice arise. With the transition from 'negative' to 'positive' integration, the balance shifts from output to input legitimation. For the citizens, actively influencing the nature and content of policies and laws becomes all the more important as discontent with public services grows.[74] Thus the logic of this development would imply that national citizens who *have* to accept a redistribution of the burdens across national borders would also *want* to exercise democratic influence in their role as EU citizens over what their heads of government negotiate or agree upon in a legal grey area. Instead of this, we see the governments engaging in delaying tactics and the populations being led by populist sentiment to a wholesale rejection of the European project. The immediate reason for this self-destructive behaviour is that the political elites and the media are reluctant to win over the populations to a common European future.

Under the pressure of the financial markets, it has become an accepted fact that an essential economic precondition for the constitutional project was neglected when the euro was introduced. Analysts agree that the European Union can withstand the financial speculation only if it acquires the necessary political steering capacities to work towards a convergence of the member states' economic and social development in the medium term at least in core Europe, i.e. among the members of the European monetary zone.[75] All of those involved

---

[74] Fritz W. Scharpf, *Governing in Europe: Effective and Democratic?* (Oxford: Oxford University Press, 1999).

[75] On the legal possibilities of a European internal differentiation, see Daniel Thym, 'Variable Geometrie in der Europäischen Union: Kontrollierte

are actually aware that this level of 'increased cooperation' is impossible within the frame of the existing
treaties. The conclusion that a joint 'economic government' is necessary, with which even the German federal
government is now reconciling itself, would mean that
European policies designed to promote the competitiveness of all economies in the euro zone would extend far
beyond the financial sector and affect national budgets
as a whole, thus encroaching deeply on the budgetary
privilege of national parliaments. Hence, if existing law
is not to be flouted, the long overdue reform is possible only by transferring further competences from
the member states to the Union.

This point has in the meantime been grasped by the
politically influential media: 'The crisis has revealed the
weaknesses of the Lisbon Treaty, with which the EU
is ill-equipped to meet the challenges confronting it as
an economic and monetary union.'[76] The obstacles to
an amendment of the treaty are high and the decision
to overcome them would require a decisive change
in behaviour on the part of the political elites. If they
want to win over their peoples to the idea of a Europe
united by bonds of solidarity, they must abandon
their accustomed combination of public relations and

Binnendifferenzierung und Schutz vor unionsexterner Gefährdung',
in Stefan Kadelbach (ed.), *60 Jahre Integration in Europa: Variable
Geometrien und politische Verflechtung jenseits der EU* (Baden-Baden:
Nomos, 2011), pp. 117–35.
[76] Martin Winter, 'Reform der Reform', *Süddeutsche Zeitung* (18 August
2011), p. 4; see also the vigorous plea for a revision of the treaty
by Catherine Hoffmann, 'Klub der Illusionisten: Ohne gemeinsame
Finanzpolitik ist die Krise in Europa nicht zu lösen', *Süddeutsche Zeitung*
(3–4 September 2011), p. 23.

incrementalism steered by experts and brace themselves for a risky, and above all inspired, struggle within the broad public. And, paradoxically, they would have to strive for something in the common European weal that runs counter to their own interest in maintaining power. For, in the long run, the scope for action at the national level would become narrower and the importance of the appearances of national potentates on the political stage would diminish.[77] On 22 July 2011, Angela Merkel and Nicolas Sarkozy agreed on a compromise, which is vague and certainly in need of interpretation, between German economic liberalism and French etatism which reflects a completely different intention. All signs point to the fact that the two leaders want to expand the executive federalism implicit in the Lisbon Treaty into a form of intergovernmental rule by the European Council, moreover, one which is at odds with the spirit of the treaty. Such a regime of central steering by the European Council would enable them to transfer the imperatives of the markets to the national budgets. This would involve using threats of sanctions and pressure on the disempowered national parliaments to enforce non-transparent and informal agreements. In this way, the heads of government would invert the European project into its opposite. The first transnational democracy would be transformed into an arrangement for exercising a kind of post-democratic, bureaucratic rule.

The alternative is to continue the democratic legal

---

[77] On the overdue politicization, see Pieter de Wilde and Michael Zürn, 'Somewhere along the line: can the politicization of European integration be reversed?', unpublished MS, 2011.

domestication of the European Union in a consistent way. A Europe-wide civic solidarity cannot develop if social inequalities between the member states become permanent structural features, and hence reinforce the fault lines separating rich and poor nations. The Union must guarantee what the Basic Law of the German Federal Republic calls the 'uniformity of living standards' (Art. 106, para. 3). This 'uniformity' refers only to a range of variation in social living conditions which is still acceptable from the perspective of distributive justice, not to the levelling of cultural differences. A political integration backed by social welfare is necessary if the national diversity and the incomparable cultural wealth of the biotope 'old Europe' are to enjoy any protection against becoming levelled in the midst of rapidly progressing globalization.

III   From the international to the cosmopolitan community

The narrative of the civilizing power of democratic legal domestication across national borders derives its impetus from a paralysing constellation in international politics whose chief current reflection is the fact that the financial markets have developed beyond the control of even the most powerful nation states. In the current crisis, the markets seem to leave no attractive options open to the state guarantors of public welfare.[78] In this situation, the attempt by the European

---

[78] In their article 'Die nächste Stufe der Krise', Jens Beckert and Wolfgang

states to recover a portion of their capacity for political self-regulation by forming a supranational community is more than a matter of mere self-assertion. This is why the narrative which I have proposed for European unification finds its extension in ideas for a politically constituted world society. At the European level, as we have seen, two innovations have proven to be ground-breaking: on the one hand, the subordination under European Union law of the member states which enjoy a monopoly on the means for a legitimate use of force and, on the other, the sharing of sovereignty between the 'citizens' and the 'peoples' as the constitution-founding subjects. Traces of the first of these two elements can be found both in the global effects of coercive international law and within the institutional framework of the United Nations. The second element could lend sharper contours to the proposals to constitute a global parliament.

However, we must not blur the distinctions between the two complementary branches of the evolution of supranational law since 1945. The supranational political community of the European Union shares with traditional states the particularism through which political units demarcate themselves from the each other in social space. In the case of a cosmopolitan association of world citizens, by contrast, only an internal perspective would remain, as already with the existing international

Streeck discuss the expected costs of the four remaining viable strategies for overcoming the sovereign debt crisis: (1) cuts in government spending, (2) tax increases, (3) suspension of debt servicing and negotiations with creditors over debt relief and (4) inflationary policy (*Frankfurter Allgemeine Zeitung* [20 August 2011], p. 29).

community of states. This shift in perspective from classical international law to the political constitution of world society is no longer a purely intellectual construction. Social reality is itself imposing this shift in perspective on contemporary consciousness. To the extent that the functional subsystems of the emerging world society reach through national borders, external costs are being generated on an unprecedented scale, and as a result a need for regulation which overtaxes existing political capacities for concerted action. That holds not only for the imbalances of the economic subsystem and the speculation which has been accelerating unchecked since the 2008 financial crisis. Environmental imbalances and the risks generated by large-scale technology have given rise to a similar global need for regulation. Today it is not individual states or coalitions of states which are confronted with such problems of the world society but politics in the singular.

Politics no longer encounters social problems only within the institutional framework of nation states but, insofar as these problems have a cross-border character, as objects of intergovernmental regulations. After two or three decades of unprecedented creativity and destructiveness of a politically intended globalization, the relation between politics and society as such is up for discussion. The global political agenda is no longer dominated in the first instance by conflicts between states but by a new theme, namely, whether the international potential for conflict can be brought under control to such an extent that globally effective norms and procedures, and correspondingly extensive political capacities for joint action, can develop out of an – until now improbable – cooperation among the major powers. Is a rhythm of development being repeated over the course of the constitutionalization of international law which became familiar over the course of European unification – namely, from the pacification of belligerent states to the institutionalized cooperation among domesticated states? In what follows I will first discuss the core functions of the United Nations, namely, peacekeeping and human rights policy (1), and then consider how an arrangement for solving the most urgent problems of a global domestic politics might look (2).

Today, the United *Nations* is a *supranational* organization comprising 193 states. A *transnational* level with a large number of international organizations has developed between the supranational and the national level (e.g. important subsidiary organizations and agencies of the UN such as the WHO, ILO, UNHCR, UNESCO, etc., and the major world economic organizations like the WTO, the IMF and the World Bank, as well as informal political steering instruments such as the periodic summits of the G-7, G-8 and G-20).[79] If we assume that the national actors, in whose hands the political decision-making powers are still basically concentrated, are not equal to the regulatory needs of the functionally differentiated world society, we arrive at plausible desiderata for the global, on the one hand, and for the transnational level, on the other.[80]

---

[79] Michael Zürn, 'Global governance as multi-level governance', in Henrik Enderlein, Sonja Wälti and Michael Zürn (eds), *Handbook on Multi-Level Governance* (Cheltenham: Edward Elgar, 2010), pp. 80–99.

[80] Jürgen Habermas, 'The constitutionalization of international law and the

From international to cosmopolitan community

The United Nations should be reorganized as a politically constituted community of states *and* citizens and at the same time should be restricted to the core tasks of peacekeeping and of the global implementation of human rights. It should acquire the necessary institutional means to fulfil these two tasks effectively and even-handedly through a corresponding reform of the Security Council and of the Courts. A further desideratum is even more difficult to satisfy – namely, constructing a negotiation system normatively integrated into the world community to address the pressing problems of a future global domestic politics (the environment and climate change, the worldwide risks of large-scale technology, regulating financial market-driven capitalism, and especially the distributional problems that arise in the trade, labour, health and transportation regimes of a highly stratified world society). For such an institution there is wanting for the present not only the political will but also the actors capable of operating globally who, in virtue of a legitimate mandate and their ability to implement agreements on a broad scale, would be suitable members of such a representative institution (whose outline is scarcely discernible in precursors such as the G-20).

The historically unprecedented construct of the EU would fit seamlessly into the contours of a politically constituted world society, which I will briefly outline. Indeed, this political world order could be construed in turn as a continuation of the democratic legal

legitimation problems of a constitution for world society', in *Europe: The Faltering Project*, pp. 109–30.

domestication of the substantive core of state power. *For the constellation of the three foundation stones of a democratic community would undergo a further change at the global level.*[81]

(1) The goal of a democratic constitution of world society calls for the creation of a community of *world citizens* – already for conceptual reasons relating to the construction of modern legal systems founded on subjective rights. The figure of thought of a *constitution-building cooperation between citizens and states* developed with reference to the example of the European Union shows how the existing international community of *states* could be complemented by the community of world citizens so that it develops into a *cosmopolitan* community.[82] The latter would not constitute itself as a world republic, however, but as a supranational association of citizens and peoples in such a way that the member states retain control over the means for a legitimate use of force, though not the right to use them as they please. The nation states would constitute the second constitution-founding

---

[81] Drawing on Hans Kelsen's unitary concept of international law, I assume a unified global legal order, which is of course itself complex. According to this, 'sovereignty' signifies a competence conferred on the state by the international community which must be exercised dutifully; the state safeguards human rights on its territory. This is also how the concept is used in the Millennium Declaration of the UN General Assembly.

[82] Daniele Archibugi and David Held (eds), *Cosmopolitan Democracy: An Agenda for a New World Order* (Cambridge: Polity, 1995); Daniele Archibugi, *The Global Commonwealth of Citizens: Toward Cosmopolitan Democracy* (Princeton, NJ: Princeton University Press, 2008); Garrett Wallace Brown and David Held (eds), *The Cosmopolitan Reader* (Cambridge: Polity, 2010).

subject of the world community alongside the world citizens. For the cosmopolitan citizens have, or would have, in turn good reasons to insist on a constitutive role of their states on all supranational levels. Insofar as citizens have already realized an element of institutionally consolidated political justice in these historical formations, they can have good reasons for wanting their nation states to survive as collective entities on the respectively higher levels of organization.

The composition of a General Assembly comprising representatives of the citizens and the states would ensure that the competing justice perspectives of world citizens, on the one hand, and of national citizens, on the other, would be taken into account and brought into balance. Already today the egalitarian reasons of the *world citizens*, who insist on equal opportunity and equal distribution, confront the relatively conservative reasons of *national citizens*, who insist on maintaining the freedoms they already enjoy at the national level (and who oppose the destruction of the exemplary *patterns* of participation founded on the welfare state; if necessary, that would not exclude a partial decrease in their own level of welfare). The competition between these two perspectives derives its justification from a historical disparity in development from which, even if it were to be gradually overcome, global domestic politics cannot simply abstract. The world parliament would have to take this twofold perspective into account especially in its role as the body responsible for the legal interpretation and development of the UN Charter.

Apart from its competences within the organizational

framework of the United Nations (especially when it comes to convening and monitoring the Security Council or global courts),[83] a rejuvenated General Assembly, in developing the Charter, the human rights agreements and international law further, would have the task of defining *binding* minimum standards which

- form the statutory basis for the human rights policy and peacekeeping of the Security Council and of the global administration of justice;
- bind the nation states in concretizing the civil rights to be accorded their citizens; and
- impose normative constraints on the robust competition for power at the transitional level when it comes to global domestic political decisions.

The organizational core, hence the second component of the world organization, would contract and simultaneously operate more effectively if the United Nations concentrated on its core business – the global enforcement of human rights and the prohibition of violence. The world organization would be subdivided and built in such a way that it could achieve its limited but fundamental ordering functions, specifically:

- the defence of international peace in the sense of a global, even-handed and effective enforcement of the prohibition of violence;

---

[83] Armin von Bogdandy and Ingo Venzke, 'In whose name? An investigation of international courts' public authority and its democratic justification', available online: http://papers.ssrn.com/sol3/papers.cfm?abstract_id=1593543 (accessed September 2011).

- taking constructive measures to protect internal order within failing states; and
- monitoring the domestic enforcement of human rights throughout the world, as well as actively protecting populations against criminal governments, whereby
- humanitarian interventions include the obligation to build sustainable and functional infrastructures.

If the implementation of UN decisions is supposed to assume the form of legal interventions, then humanitarian law must also be developed into a *police law* which is in accordance with the rule of law and is tailored to military necessities.

Since the world community itself is not supposed to assume the character of a state, it has to rely on the fact that the national monopolists on the legitimate use of force submit to the (judicially monitored) decisions of the Security Council. That states (or regional defensive alliances) place their military potential at the service of the world organization is an expression of the shift in the relationship between national sanctioning power and law which has begun at the UN level and has already been accomplished in the European Union. With the change in attitudes on the part of member states, which are beginning to see themselves no longer as 'sovereign' powers but as *members* of the international community united by bonds of solidarity, the process of civilizing the exercise of political authority would continue on a higher level.

Of course, it still holds true that bringing the politics of the United Nations under the sway of democratic legislation calls for an improbable feedback loop between the world parliament and the opinion- and will-formation of world citizens who would be periodically called to the polls. However, empirical reasons speak against the expectation that a still more fluid civic solidarity will undergo a global expansion.[84] For example, the attention of global public opinion – in spite of the stimuli provided by globally operating non-governmental organizations – is sparked only intermittently by this or that major event without achieving structural permanence. However, the scepticism is directed not only at the limited capability of the actually emerging global public opinion in which Kant already invested his cosmopolitan hopes. At this point, communitarian doubts that popular sovereignty can be transnationalized *also* resurface – and, when it comes to the global level, not altogether without good reason. For here a connection between world citizens via the circuits of communication of the global public sphere is *no longer embedded in the context of a shared political culture*. The transnational extension of civic solidarity, which we can still reckon with in the case of a *territorially restricted* union of citizens and states shaped by common historical experiences, comes to nothing, as it were, when it is supposed to assume a global format.

Any political community, no matter how large and

[84] Patrizia Nanz and Jens Steffek, 'Zivilgesellschaftliche Partizipation und die Demokratisierung internationalen Regierens', in Niesen and Herborth (eds), *Anarchie der kommunikativen Freiheit*, pp. 87–110. A somewhat more encouraging picture emerges from the secondary analysis of Michael Zürn, 'Vier Modelle einer globalen Ordnung in kosmopolitischer Absicht', *Politische Vierteljahresschrift* 1 (2011): 78–118, here especially pp. 100ff.

pluralistic it may be, can differentiate itself from its environments with reference to an intersubjectively shared political culture. This is why democratic elections are the result of a shared practice of opinion- and will-formation, which is normally marked by the self-reference to the 'we' of a particular, *because limited*, community. The election to a world parliament would be the only *entirely inclusive* process of this kind in which a certain type of theme would have to be absent – namely, themes of *self-demarcation and self-assertion*. In political election campaigns, questions touching on a common ethos – for example, the level of security of nuclear power stations or the level of demands that an education, health or transport system should satisfy – are always implicitly mingled with an element of self-assertion. The collectivity of the present-day generations of human beings scattered across the globe certainly also shares abstract interests in basic goods necessary for survival (such as protecting ecological equilibriums and natural resources or preventing extensive nuclear contamination). But world citizens do not form a collective that would be held together by a political interest in the *self-assertion* of a way of life that shapes their identity. Such abstract interests in survival could acquire a *political character*, therefore, only if they were to lose their abstract character and, in the context of a particular form of life, enter into competition with other interests of other forms of life.

But is this also true of the two interests whose protection is the responsibility of the cosmopolitan community? Isn't it different in the case of the interest in preventing war and violence and in implementing civil rights? Isn't this a matter of *a fortiori* 'general' interests which are 'depoliticized' to such an extent that they are 'shared' by the world population beyond all political-cultural divisions – and, when they are violated, are judged exclusively from the *moral point of view*? We are inherently familiar with everyday situations in which we feel obliged to show solidarity with strangers, with everything that has a human face, without any hint of self-assertion. Only this moral universe of all persons who act responsibly – Kant's 'kingdom of ends' – is entirely inclusive: no one is excluded. Injustice that is perpetrated against *any* person, the injury suffered by a person *whoever they may be*, irks our moral sensibility and goads us on to moral indignation or to assistance. These sentiments fuel moral judgements which, assuming that reciprocal perspective-taking leads to a sufficiently decentred perception of the conflict and to an even-handed consideration of all affected interests, can be justified in reasonable terms.

On the other hand, when it comes to the tasks of the United Nations, we are not speaking simply of morality but of law and politics. Law must step in wherever a moral division of labour becomes necessary because individual judgements and motivations are not sufficient.[85] Interestingly enough, however, precisely in the policy areas to which the United Nations should confine itself – human rights and the prohibition of violence – legal norms of a special kind find application, namely, ones which can be justified exclusively in moral

---

[85] Jürgen Habermas, *Between Facts and Norms*, trans. William Rehg (Cambridge: Polity, 1996), pp. 118ff.

terms. Irrespective of their legal form, these overriding subjective rights have an exclusively moral content because human rights circumscribe precisely that part of universalistic morality which can be translated into the medium of coercive law.[86] This explains the *judicial rather than political nature* of the decisions that would be taken within the context of the reformed United Nations as we conceive it. The world parliament would conduct debates over background conditions of global justice and the Security Council would take momentous, but substantially justiciable, decisions that could be monitored by courts.

A fortunate consequence of the restriction to legal, but fundamentally moral matters is a deflation of the demands on legitimation of the world organization. For the relevant principles of distributive justice as well as the negative duties to refrain from justiciable human rights violations and wars of aggression are rooted in the core moral contents of all of the major world religions and in the cultures they have shaped. These intuitively known norms permit every world citizen to make a morally informed judgement about the work of the organs of the world organization because the latter have to justify their decisions in terms of corresponding standards – standards which have acquired greater precision through judicial elaboration. In view of the thus *reduced legitimacy requirement*, world citizens need not be expected to engage in collective will-formation in the essentially political sense. The elections to the world

---

[86] On this, see my essay 'The Concept of Human Dignity and the Realistic Utopia of Human Rights' in this volume (pp. 71–100).

parliament would only express the in essence morally justified 'yes' or 'no' to the supranational application of *presumptively shared* moral principles and norms.

To sum up, it can then be asserted regarding the global level at which the world organization will operate that the chain of legitimacy could extend without interruption from national states via regional regimes such as the European Union to the world organization, if we may assume:

- that the *international* community will be *extended* to form a *cosmopolitan* community via the representation of *world citizens* based on elections;
- that the competences of the United Nations are *restricted* to the key tasks of maintaining order which have a moral content and are legal in nature; and
- that the global, in part digitally produced, communication processes extend beyond porous national public spheres in such a way as to enable all peoples to form a reasoned judgement about the moral core content of decisions taken at the UN level.

(2) However, the chain of legitimacy described relates only to the *security-relevant* tasks of the world organization. The fact that the United Nations is relieved of the issues of world domestic politics, which are political in the narrower sense of being *relevant for distribution*, has a reverse side.[87] In our design, the actors

---

[87] Here I leave to one side the important domain of the international organizations which coordinate state activities in 'technical' issues, i.e. ones which are not relevant for distribution policy.

capable of acting globally comprise the 'natural' 'world powers' as well as those constructed through supranational integration, where the latter would ideally be representative of all sectors of the world society. The compromises which these actors are supposed to negotiate at *the transnational level* resist being subjected to democratic legal control in the manner of the European Union as long as the corresponding negotiation system is based exclusively on international treaties. According to classical international law, in foreign policy matters governments enjoy the prerogative of concluding international treaties which are subject to democratic participation and legitimation to a much lesser extent than the domestic politics monitored by parliament.[88] This weak, at best indirect, legitimation is also at first sight characteristic of the world domestic politics which must be negotiated transnationally. If the chain of democratic legitimation were to break off at this point, however, the proposed design would not be able to satisfy its claim concerning the unity of a global legal order which lowers the threshold between international and national law.

The weakness in legitimacy by comparison with a fully developed European Union is a result of the fact that global domestic politics is supposed to be left to the negotiations between global players without the direct participation of the world parliament and not to be conducted *simultaneously by states and world citizens represented by parliament*, on an analogy with the 'ordinary legislative procedure'. In our model, however,

[88] See Christoph Möllers, *Die drei Gewalten*, pp. 155ff.

67

the transnational relations between the global players to whom global domestic politics would be entrusted would *not* remain intact along the lines of traditional international law. For the point on which the proposed design turns is that the political process above the level of states and unions of states is supposed to be split into *two different policy fields* and to branch into *corresponding strands of legitimation*. According to this design, the tasks of global security and human rights policy fall within the competence of a world organization which is composed in such a way that, all things considered, the lowered legitimacy requirement in its policy areas could be satisfied. The tasks of world domestic politics with distributive implications are not included in this hierarchically constructed arrangement of competences. They are diverted into a transnational negotiation system whose decisions, although they would have a weaker legitimation, would by no means be abandoned *exclusively* to the play of international power dynamics.

For this political process, which is as it were confined to the horizontal level, is also supposed to remain *embedded in the context of the constituted world society* – not only because the world organization would oversee the factual balance of power and the appropriate representation of every state in the transnational negotiating body. More important are two additional reasons. First, the transnational negotiations would be conducted by *the same* actors who would make their military forces available at the supranational level for enforcing the peacekeeping and human rights policies which they would be involved in designing. In this sense they would also have to regard themselves as members of the cosmopolitan community. Therefore, it is all the more likely, second, that the transnational negations would be conducted within the confines of the standard of justice which the world parliament continually adapts with a view to the level of duties of protection laid down by human rights.

These arguments are not sufficient, however, to fill the gap in parliamentary accountability in the chain of democratic juridification of a future world domestic politics *completely*. However, this gap is the result of the historical fact that the demanding condition of 'uniform living conditions' throughout the world cannot be fulfilled for the time being. This circumstance must be assessed in political and not exclusively in moral terms once the world organization takes the temporal dimension into consideration and places world domestic politics under an obligation to establish a more socially just world order *in the medium term*. Every moral sentiment bristles against the monstrous injustice of a highly stratified world society in which even elementary basic goods and life chances are today unevenly distributed in an intolerable way.[89] But any design of a world order aiming at civilizing the exercise of political authority, no matter how farsighted it may be, must take account of the fact that the historical asynchronicity of regional developments and the corresponding socio-economic disparities between the multiple modernities cannot be erased *overnight*.

[89] David Held and Ayse Kaya (eds), *Global Inequality: Patterns and Explanations* (Cambridge: Polity, 2007).

Today we are witnessing a shift in the balance of economic power in world politics which, in the midst of the 2008 financial crisis, forced the club of leading industrial nations to expand into the group of the G-20 nations. This overdue step was intended finally to combine efforts to build institutions and establish procedures through which problems of an in any case inescapable future world domestic politics would assume a workable form under the inexorable destructive pressure of the financial markets. We do not lack the moral standards in terms of which we can today assess the prevailing economic and social structures or confront existing institutions and established practices with demands for more 'global justice'.[90] However, a philosophical discussion about justice without practical consequences would acquire political relevance only when it could no longer be conducted just in academia but instead in a world parliament which, in virtue of being composed of states and citizens, *would take into account the factor of time relevant for justice*. As is already the case today in the EU (albeit within different time horizons), in the world community the justice perspectives of both of the constituent subjects – the egalitarian yardsticks of world citizens and the conservative yardsticks of the member states, which currently differ according to levels of development – would then tend to converge as concerted political action gave rise to a factual assimilation of living standards.

---

[90] Thomas Pogge (ed.), *Global Justice* (Oxford: Blackwell, 2001); Amartya Sen, *The Idea of Justice* (Cambridge, MA: Harvard University Press, 2009).

The Concept of Human Dignity and the Realistic Utopia of Human Rights

Article 1 of the Universal Declaration of Human Rights, which was adopted by the United Nations on 10 December 1948, begins with the statement: 'All human beings are born free and equal in dignity and rights.'[1] The Preamble also speaks of human dignity and human rights in the same breath. It reaffirms the 'faith in fundamental human rights, in the dignity and worth of the human person'.[2] The Basic Law of the Federal Republic of Germany, which was enacted sixty years ago, begins with a section on basic rights. Article 1 of this section opens with the statement: 'Human dignity is inviolable'. Prior to this, similar formulations appeared in five out of eight of the German state constitutions enacted between 1946 and 1949. Nowadays human dignity also

---

[1] The first sentence of the Preamble calls at the same time for recognition of the 'inherent dignity' and 'equal and inalienable rights of all members of the human family'.

[2] '[T]he peoples of the United Nations have in the Charter reaffirmed their faith in fundamental human rights, in the dignity and worth of the human person . . .'

features prominently in human rights discourse and in judicial decision-making.[3]

The inviolability of human dignity became the focus of public attention in Germany in 2006 when the Federal Constitutional Court declared the 'Aviation Security Act' enacted by the Bundestag to be unconstitutional. At the time, the parliament was thinking of the '9/11' scenario – in other words, the terrorist attack on the Twin Towers of the World Trade Center; the intention of the bill was to authorize the armed forces in such a situation to shoot down passenger aircraft which had been transformed into missiles in order to avert the threat to an indeterminately large number of people on the ground. According to the court, however, the killing of the passengers by agencies of the state would be unconstitutional. It argued that the duty of the state (according to Art. 2.2 GG)[4] to protect the lives of the potential victims of a terrorist attack is secondary to the duty to respect the human dignity of the passengers: '. . . with their lives being disposed of unilaterally by the state, the persons on board the aircraft . . . are denied the value which is due to a human being for his or her own sake.'[5] These words of the court unmistakably re-echo Kant's categorical imperative. The respect for the

---

[3] Erhard Denninger, 'Der Menschenwürdesatz im Grundgesetz und seine Entwicklung in der Verfassungsrechtsprechung', in Franz-Josef Peine and Heinrich A. Wolf (eds), *Nachdenken über Eigentum: Festschrift für Alexander von Brünneck* (Baden-Baden: Nomos, 2011), pp. 397–411.

[4] 'Every person has the right to life and physical integrity.'

[5] BVerfG, 1 BvR 357/05, 15 February 2006, para. 124; on this judgement, see Jochen von Bernstorff, 'Pflichtenkollision und Menschenwürdegarantie: Zum Vorrang staatlicher Achtungspflichten im Normbereich von Art. 1 GG', *Der Staat* 47 (2008): 21–40.

dignity of every person forbids the state to dispose over any individual merely as a means to another end, even if that end be to save the lives of many other people.

It is an interesting fact that it was only after the end of the Second World War that the philosophical concept of human dignity, which already existed in antiquity and acquired its current canonical expression in Kant, found its way into texts of international law and into the national constitutions that came into force in the postwar period. Only during the past decades has it also played a central role in international jurisdiction. By contrast, the concept of human dignity is to be found as a legal concept neither in the classical eighteenth-century human rights declarations nor in the codifications of the nineteenth century.[6] Why did the notion of 'human rights' find its way into the law so much earlier than that of 'human dignity'? To be sure, the founding documents of the United Nations, which make the connection between human rights and human dignity explicit, were clearly a response to the mass crimes committed under the Nazi regime and to the massacres of the Second World War. Does this in addition account for the prominent place also accorded human dignity in the German, Italian and Japanese postwar constitutions, hence in the constitutions of the successor regimes of the authors of this twentieth-century moral catastrophe and their allies? Does the idea of *human rights* become, as it were, retrospectively morally charged – and possibly

---

[6] See Christopher McCrudden, 'Human dignity and judicial interpretation of human rights', *European Journal of International Law* 19 (2008): 655–724.

over-charged – with the concept of *human dignity* only against the historical background of the Holocaust?

The recent career of the concept of 'human dignity' in constitutional and international legal discussions tends to support these ideas. There is just one exception from the mid-nineteenth century. In the negotiations over the abolition of the death penalty and of corporal punishment in paragraph 139 of the German Constitution of March 1849, we find the statement: 'A free people must respect human dignity even in the case of a criminal.'[7] However, this constitution, which was the product of the first bourgeois revolution in Germany, never came into force. One way or the other, the temporal dislocation between the history of human rights dating back to the seventeenth century and the relatively recent currency of the concept of human dignity in codifications of national and international law and in the administration of justice over the past half-century remains a striking fact.

Contrary to the assumption that the concept of human rights became morally charged by that of human dignity only in retrospect, I would like to defend the thesis that a close conceptual connection existed, if at first only implicitly, from the very beginning. The origin of human rights has always been resistance to despotism, oppression and humiliation. Today nobody can utter these venerable articles – for example, the proposition: 'No one shall be subjected to torture or to cruel, inhuman or degrading treatment or punishment' (Art. 5 of the Universal Declaration) – without hearing the

---

[7] Denninger, 'Der Menschenwürdesatz im Grundgesetz', p. 397.

echo of the outcry of countless tortured and murdered human creatures that resonates in them. The appeal to human rights feeds off the outrage of the humiliated at the violation of their human dignity. If this forms the historical starting point, traces of a conceptual connection between human dignity and human rights should be evident from early on in the development of law itself. Thus we must first answer the question of whether 'human dignity' signifies a substantive normative basic concept from which human rights can be deduced by specifying the conditions under which they are violated. Or is the expression merely an empty formula which summarizes a catalogue of individual, disparate and unrelated human rights?

I will present some legal reasons in support of the claim that 'human dignity' is not a retrospective classificatory expression, an empty placeholder, as it were, that lumps a multiplicity of different phenomena together, but the moral 'source'[8] from which all of the basic rights derive their sustenance (1). I will go on to present a systematic analysis, in the guise of a conceptual history, of the catalytic role played by the concept of dignity in the construction of human rights out of rational morality and the form of law (2). Finally, the origin of human rights in the moral notion of human dignity explains the explosive political force of a concrete utopia which I would like to defend against the blanket dismissal of human rights (Carl Schmitt), on the one hand, and

---

[8] 'The inviolability of the dignity of the person is the source of all basic rights', is how it is put, for example, in Article 14, paragraph 2, of the constitution of the Free State of Saxony of 1992.

against more recent attempts to blunt their radical thrust, on the other (3).

(1) Because of their abstract character, basic rights need to be spelled out in concrete terms in each particular case. In the process, lawmakers and judges often arrive at different results in different cultural contexts; today this is apparent, for example, in the regulation of controversial ethical issues such as assisted suicide, abortion and genetic enhancement. Equally uncontroversial is that, because of this need for interpretation, universal legal concepts facilitate negotiated compromises. Thus appealing to the concept of human dignity undoubtedly made it easier to reach an overlapping consensus among parties from different cultures at the founding of the United Nations, for example, and more generally when negotiating human rights agreements and international legal conventions: 'Everyone could agree that human dignity was central, but not why or how.'[9]

In spite of this observation, the juridical meaning of human dignity is not exhausted by its function as a smokescreen for disguising more profound differences. The fact that the concept of 'human dignity' has also occasionally facilitated compromises when specifying and extending human rights by neutralizing unbridgeable differences cannot explain its belated emergence *as* a legal concept. I would like to show that changing historical conditions have merely thematized and made us aware of something that was inscribed in human rights implicitly

---

[9] McCrudden, 'Human dignity and judicial interpretation of human rights', p. 678.

from the outset, namely, the normative substance of the equal dignity of every human being that human rights only spell out. Thus judges appeal to the protection of human dignity, for example, when the unforeseen risks of new invasive technologies lead them to introduce a right to informational autonomy. The Federal Constitutional Court took a similar line in its groundbreaking decision of 9 February 2010 on the assessment of benefits entitlements in accordance with SGB II (Second Book of the Code of Social Law), section 20, paragraph 2 (unemployment benefit II).[10] It took this occasion to 'derive' a basic right to a minimum income from Article 1 of the German Constitution that enables the beneficiaries (and their children) to enjoy an appropriate 'participation in social, cultural and political life'.[11]

The experience of the violation of human dignity fulfils an inventive function in many cases, be it in view of the unbearable social conditions and the marginalization of impoverished social classes, or in view of the unequal treatment of women and men in the workplace or of discrimination against foreigners and against cultural, linguistic, religious and racial minorities, or in view of the ordeal of young women from immigrant families who have to liberate themselves from the violence of a traditional code of honour, or in view of the brutal expulsion of illegal immigrants and asylum seekers. In the light of historical challenges, *different* aspects of the meaning of human dignity acquire urgency and

---

[10] BVerfG, 1 BvL 1/09 of 9 February 2010. English translation available online: www.bundesverfassungsgericht.de/entscheidungen/ls201002 09_1bvl000109en.html (accessed 11 October 2011).

[11] Ibid., paragraph 135.

relevance in each case. These features of human dignity specified and actualized on different occasions can then lead both to a more complete exhaustion of the normative substance of existing civil rights and to the discovery and construction of *new* ones.[12] Through this process the background intuition of humiliation forces its way first into the consciousness of suffering individuals and then into the legal texts, where it finds conceptual articulation and elaboration.

The 1919 Constitution of the German Reich, which pioneered the introduction of social rights, provides an example of this incremental development. In Article 151 the text speaks of 'achieving a dignified life for everyone'. Here the concept of human dignity remains concealed behind the adjectival use of a colloquial expression; but as early as 1944 the International Labour Organization (ILO) employed the rhetoric of human dignity without qualification in a similar context.[13] Moreover, just a few years later Article 22 of the Universal Declaration of Human Rights already calls for guarantees of economic, social and cultural rights, so that every individual can live under conditions which are 'indispensable for his dignity and the free development of his personality'.[14]

---

[12] McCrudden speaks in similar cases of 'justifying the creation of new, and the extension of existing, rights' ('Human dignity and judicial interpretation of human rights', p. 721).

[13] Paragraph 2a of the declaration concerning the aims and purposes of the International Labour Organization, adopted on 10 May 1944 in Philadelphia, states that: 'all human beings, irrespective of race, creed or sex, have the right to pursue both their material well-being and their spiritual development in conditions of freedom and dignity, of economic security and equal opportunity.'

[14] 'Everyone, as a member of society, has the right to social security and is entitled to realization, through national effort and international

Since that time we speak of successive 'generations' of human rights. The heuristic function of human dignity also provides the key to the logical interconnections between these four categories of rights. Only *in collaboration* with each other can basic rights fulfil the moral promise to respect the human dignity of every person *equally*.[15]

The *liberal rights*, which crystallize around the inviolability and security of the person, around free commerce and the unhindered exercise of religion, are designed to prevent the intrusion of the state into the private sphere. They constitute, together with the *democratic rights of participation*, the package of so-called classical civil rights. In fact, however, the citizens have equal opportunities to make use of these rights only when they simultaneously enjoy guarantees of a sufficient level of independence in their private and economic lives and when they are able to form their personal identities in the cultural environment of their choice. Experiences of exclusion, suffering and discrimination teach us that classical civil rights acquire 'equal value' (Rawls) for all citizens only when they are supplemented by *social and cultural rights*. The claims to an appropriate share in the prosperity and culture of society as a whole place narrow limits on the scope for shifting *systemic* costs

---

co-operation and in accordance with the organization and resources of each State, of the economic, social and cultural rights indispensable for his dignity and the free development of his personality.'

[15] Georg Lohmann, 'Die Menschenrechte: Unteilbar und gleichgewichtig? – Eine Skizze', in Georg Lohmann, Stefan Gosepath, Arnd Pollmann, Claudia Mahler and Norman Weiß, *Die Menschenrechte: Unteilbar und gleichgewichtig?*, Studien zu Grund- und Menschenrechten 11 (Potsdam: Universitätsverlag Potsdam, 2005), pp. 5–20.

and risks onto the shoulders of individuals. These claims set constraints on the increase in social inequality and forbid the exclusion of entire groups from social and cultural life as a whole. Thus policies such as those which have predominated in recent decades not only in the United States and Great Britain but also in continental Europe, and indeed throughout the world – i.e. ones which pretend to be able to secure an autonomous life for citizens *primarily* through guarantees of economic liberties – tend to destroy the balance between the different categories of basic rights. Human dignity, which is one and the same everywhere and for everyone, grounds the *indivisibility* of all categories of human rights.

This development also explains the conspicuousness that this concept has acquired in the administration of justice. The more deeply civil rights suffuse the legal system as a whole, the more often their influence extends beyond the vertical relation between individual citizens and the state and permeates the horizontal relations among individuals and groups. The result is an increase in the frequency of collisions which call for a balancing of competing claims founded upon basic rights.[16] A justified decision in such hard cases is often made possible only by an appeal to a violation of human dignity whose absolute validity grounds a claim to priority. In judicial discourse, therefore, the role of this concept is far from that of a vague placeholder for a missing integral

---

[16] The discussion concerning the so-called horizontal effect [*Drittwirkung*] of basic rights, which has been conducted in Europe over the past half-century, has recently also found an echo in the United States; see Stephen Gardbaum, 'The "horizontal effect" of constitutional rights', *Michigan Law Review* 102 (2003): 388–459.

conception of human rights. 'Human dignity' performs the function of a seismograph that registers what is constitutive for a democratic legal order – namely, just those rights that the citizens of a political community must grant themselves if they are to be able to respect one another as members of a voluntary association of free and equal persons. The guarantee of these human rights first gives rise to the status of citizens who have a claim as subjects of equal rights to be respected in their human dignity.

After two hundred years of modern constitutional history, we have a better grasp of what set this development apart from the beginning: human dignity forms the 'portal' through which the egalitarian and universalistic substance of morality is imported into law. The idea of human dignity is the conceptual hinge which connects the morality of equal respect for everyone with positive law and democratic lawmaking in such a way that their interplay could give rise to a political order founded upon human rights, given suitable historical conditions. To be sure, the classical human rights declarations, when they speak of 'inborn' or 'inalienable' rights, of 'inherent' or 'natural' rights, or of *droits inaliénables et sacrés*, betray their religious and metaphysical origins ('We hold these Truths to be self-evident, that all men are . . . endowed with certain unalienable rights . . .'). In the secular state, however, such predicates function primarily as placeholders; they remind us of the mode of a *generally acceptable justification* of the exacting moral content of these rights whose epistemic dimension is *beyond state control*. Moreover, the Founding Fathers recognized that human rights, notwithstanding their purely moral justification, are in need of a democratic 'Declaration' and that they must be specified and implemented within an established political community. Because the moral promise of equal respect for everybody is supposed to be cashed out in legal currency, human rights exhibit a Janus face turned simultaneously to morality and to law.[17] Notwithstanding their exclusively moral *content*, they have the *form* of positive, enforceable subjective rights which guarantee specific liberties and claims. They are designed to be *spelled out in concrete terms* through democratic legislation, to be *specified* from case to case in adjudication and to be *enforced* with public sanctions. Thus human rights circumscribe that and only that part of an enlightened morality which can be translated into the medium of coercive law and become political reality in the robust shape of effective civil rights.[18]

---

[17] Georg Lohmann, 'Menschenrechte zwischen Moral und Recht', in Stefan Gosepath and Georg Lohmann (eds), *Philosophie der Menschenrechte* (Frankfurt am Main: Suhrkamp, 1998), pp. 62–95.

[18] I do not think that this reflection requires me to revise my original introduction of the system of rights in Jürgen Habermas, *Between Facts and Norms*, ch. 3; see also 'Constitutional democracy – a paradoxical union of contradictory principles?' in *Time of Transitions*, trans. C. Cronin and M. Pensky (Cambridge: Polity, 2006), pp. 113–28. Human rights differ from moral rights, among other things, in virtue of the fact that they are geared to being institutionalized, and thus have to be produced, for which purpose they require a shared democratic process, whereas people who act morally regard themselves without further qualification as subjects who are *inherently* embedded in a network of moral duties and rights; cf. Jeffrey Flynn, 'Habermas on human rights: law, morality, and intercultural dialogue', *Social Theory and Praxis* 29 (2003): 431–57. However, at the time I failed to take account of two things. On the one hand, the cumulative experiences of violated dignity constitute a source of the moral motivation for the historically unprecedented praxis of constitution-making at the close of the eighteenth century; on the other hand, the status-creating social

(2) This at the time entirely new category of rights reunites two elements which had first become separated in the early modern period in the course of the disintegration of Christian natural law, became independent and to begin with developed in opposite directions. The result of this differentiation was, on the one side, the internalized, rationally justified morality anchored in the individual conscience, which in Kant withdraws entirely into the transcendental domain; and, on the other side, the coercive, positive, enacted law which served absolutist rulers or the traditional assemblies of estates as an instrument for constructing the institutions of the modern state and a market society. The concept of human rights is a product of an improbable synthesis of these two elements. *'Human dignity' served as a conceptual hinge in establishing this connection.* The learned concept of human dignity was itself transformed in the course of this synthesis. An important role is clearly also played by those colloquial notions of social dignity which had become associated with particular statuses in the stratified societies of medieval and early modern Europe.[19] Admittedly, the hypothesis which I am going to develop calls for more

recognition of the dignity of the other forms a conceptual bridge between the moral content of the equal recognition of everyone and the legal form of human rights. Here I leave open whether the shift in attention to these states of affairs has further consequences for my deflationary reading of the discourse principle 'D' in the justification of the basic rights; see my controversy with the objections of Karl-Otto Apel in 'On the architectonics of discursive justification: a brief response to a major controversy', in *Between Naturalism and Religion*, pp. 77–97.

[19] On the emergence of the legal concept of human dignity from the generalization of status-bound dignity, see Jeremy Waldron, 'Dignity and rank', *European Journal of Sociology* 48 (2007): 201–37.

research, both in terms of conceptual history and of the history of European revolutions.

I would like to highlight two aspects with a view to the genealogy of human rights: on the one hand, the mediating function of 'human dignity' in the shift of perspective from moral duties to legal claims (a), and, on the other hand, the paradoxical generalization of a concept of dignity that was originally geared not to any equal recognition of dignity but to *status differences* (b).

(a) The modern doctrines of morality and law which claim to rest on human reason alone share the concepts of individual autonomy and equal respect for everyone. This common foundation of morality and law often obscures the decisive difference that, whereas morality imposes duties concerning others that pervade all spheres of action without exception, modern law creates well-defined domains of private choice for the pursuit of an individual life of one's own. Under the revolutionary premise that everything is permitted which is not explicitly prohibited, subjective rights rather than duties provide the starting point for the construction of modern legal systems. The guiding principle for Hobbes and for modern law generally is that all persons are allowed to act or to refrain from acting as they wish within the confines of the law. Actors take a different perspective when, instead of *following* moral commands, they make use of their rights. A person in a *moral relation* asks herself what she owes to another person independently of her social relation to him – how well she knows him, how he behaves and what she might expect from him. People who stand in a *legal relation* to each other are concerned about potential *claims* they expect others to *make* on them. In a legal community, the first person acquires obligations only as a result of claims that a second person can make on her.[20]

Take the case of a police officer who wants to extort a confession from a suspect through the illegal threat of torture. In his role as a moral person, this threat alone, not to speak of the actual infliction of the pain, would be sufficient to give him a bad conscience, quite apart from the behaviour of the offender. By contrast, a legal relation is actualized between the police officer who is acting illegally and the individual under interrogation only when *the latter* defends herself and takes legal action to obtain her rights (or a public prosecutor reacts to the violation of the law). Naturally, in both cases the person threatened is a source of normative claims which are violated by torture. However, the fact that the actions in question violate moral norms is all that is required to give an offender a bad conscience, whereas the legal relation which is objectively violated remains latent until a claim is raised that actualizes it.

Thus Klaus Günther regards the 'transition from reciprocal moral obligations to reciprocally established and accorded rights' as an act of 'self-empowerment to self-determination'.[21] The *transition from morality to law* calls for a shift from symmetrically intertwined

---

[20] Georg Lohmann writes on this: 'A moral right counts as justified when a corresponding moral duty exists that itself counts as justified . . . a legal right when it is part of a positive legal order which can claim legitimacy as a whole' ('Menschenrechte zwischen Moral und Recht', p. 66).

[21] Georg Lohmann seems to misunderstand this transition as one from traditional to enlightened morality (ibid., p. 87).

perspectives of respect and esteem for the autonomy of *the other* to raising claims to recognition and esteem for *one's own autonomy* on the part of the other. The morally enjoined *concern* for the vulnerable other is replaced by the self-confident *demand* for legal recognition as a self-determined subject who 'lives, feels, and acts in accordance with his or her own judgement'.[22] Thus the legal recognition *claimed* by citizens reaches beyond the reciprocal moral recognition of responsible subjects; it has the concrete meaning of the respect *demanded* for a status that is *deserved*, and as such it is infused with the connotations of the 'dignity' which was associated in the past with membership in socially respected corporate bodies.

(b) The concrete concept of dignity or of 'social honour' belongs to the world of hierarchically ordered traditional societies. In those societies a person could derive his dignity and self-respect, for example, from the code of honour of the nobility, from the ethos of trade guilds or professions, or from the corporative spirit of universities. When these status-dependent dignities, which occur in the plural, coalesce into the universal dignity of 'the' human being, this new, abstract dignity sheds the particular characteristics of a corporative ethos. At the same time, this universalized dignity, which all people possess equally, also preserves the connotation of *self-respect*

[22] Klaus Günther, 'Menschenrechte zwischen Staaten und Dritten: Vom vertikalen zum horizontalen Verständnis der Menschenrechte', in Nicole Deitelhoff and Jens Steffek (eds), *Was bleibt vom Staat? Demokratie, Recht und Verfassung im globalen Zeitalter* (Frankfurt am Main: Campus, 2009), pp. 259–80, here pp. 275f.

based on *social recognition*. As such a form of social dignity, therefore, human dignity also requires anchoring in a social status, i.e. membership in an organized community in space and time. But now the status is supposed to be the same for everyone. Thus the concept of human dignity transfers the content of a morality of equal respect for everyone to the status order of citizens who derive their self-respect from being recognized by all other citizens as *subjects of equal actionable rights*.

It is not unimportant in this context that this status can be established only within the framework of a constitutional state that never arises of its own accord. Rather, this framework must be *created* by the citizens themselves *using the means of positive law* and must be protected and developed under historically changing conditions. As a modern legal concept, human dignity is associated with the status that citizens assume in the *self-created* political order. As addressees, citizens can come to enjoy the rights that protect their human dignity only by first uniting as authors of the democratic undertaking of establishing and maintaining a political order based on human rights.[23] The dignity conferred by the status of democratic citizenship is nourished by the republican appreciation of this democratic achievement

---

[23] Therefore human rights are not opposed to democracy but are co-original with it. The relation between them is one of mutual presupposition: human rights make possible the democratic process without which they themselves could not be enacted and concretized within the framework of the civil rights-based constitutional state. On the justification in terms of a theory of discourse, see Klaus Günther, 'Liberale und diskurstheoretische Deutungen der Menschenrechte', in Winfried Brugger, Ulfrid Neumann and Stephan Kirste (eds), *Rechtsphilosophie im 21. Jahrhundert* (Frankfurt am Main: Suhrkamp, 2008), pp. 338–59.

and of a corresponding orientation to the public good. This is reminiscent of the meaning that the ancient Romans associated with the word *dignitas* – namely, the prestige of statesmen and officeholders who have served the *res publica*. Of course, the distinction of the few outstanding 'dignitaries' and notabilities contrasts with the dignity guaranteed to *all* citizens *equally* by the constitutional state.

Jeremy Waldron draws attention to the paradoxical fact that the egalitarian concept of human dignity is the result of a generalization of particularistic dignities which must not entirely lose the connotation of 'fine distinctions': 'Once associated with hierarchical differentiation of rank and status, "dignity" now conveys the idea that all human persons belong to the same rank and that the rank is a very high one indeed.'[24] Waldron understands this generalization process in such a way that all citizens now acquire the highest rank possible, for example that which was once reserved for the nobility. But does this capture the meaning of the equal dignity of every human being? Even the direct precursors of the concept of human dignity in Greek philosophy, especially in the Stoics, and Roman humanism (for example, in Cicero), do not form a semantic bridge to the egalitarian meaning of the modern concept. That same period developed a sophisticated collective notion of *dignitas humana*, but it was explained in terms of a distinguished ontological status of human beings in the cosmos, of the particular rank enjoyed by human beings vis-à-vis 'lower' forms of life in virtue of species-specific

[24] Waldron, 'Dignity and rank', p. 201.

faculties such as reason and reflection. The superior value of the species might justify some kind of species protection but not the inviolability of the dignity of the individual person as a source of normative claims. Two decisive stages in the genealogy of the concept are still missing. The collective generalization first had to be joined by individualization. At issue is the *worth of the individual* in the horizontal relations between different human beings, not the status of 'human beings' in the vertical relation to God or to 'lower' creatures on the evolutionary scale. Second, the relative superiority of humanity and its members had to be replaced by the absolute worth of the person. At issue is the *unique worth* of each person. These two steps were taken in Europe when ideas from the Judeo-Christian tradition were appropriated by philosophy, a process which I would like to address briefly.[25]

A close connection was already drawn between *dignitas* and *persona* in antiquity; yet it was only in the medieval discussions of human beings' creation in the likeness to God that the individual person became liberated from its set of social roles. Everyone must face the Last Judgement as an irreplaceable and unique person. Another stage in the conceptual history of individualization is represented by the approaches in Spanish scholasticism which sought to distinguish subjective

---

[25] On the theological background of the concept of human dignity, see Tine Stein's study in the history of ideas (*Himmlische Quellen und irdisches Recht: Religiöse Voraussetzungen des freiheitlichen Verfassungsstaates* [Frankfurt am Main: Campus, 2007], especially ch. 7); see also Wolfgang Huber, *Gerechtigkeit und Recht: Grundlinien christlicher Rechtsethik* (Gütersloh: Kaiser, 1996), pp. 222–86.

rights from the objective system of natural law.[26] The decisive orientation is, however, the moralization of the understanding of individual freedom in Hugo Grotius und Samuel Pufendorf. Kant radicalized this understanding into a deontological concept of autonomy; however, the price paid for the radicality of this concept was a disembodied status of the free will in the transcendental 'kingdom of ends'. Freedom on this conception consists in the capacity to give oneself and to follow reasonable laws, reflecting generalizable values and interests. The relationship of rational beings to each other is determined by the reciprocal recognition of the legislating will of each person, where each individual should 'treat himself and all others never merely as means but always at the same time as ends in themselves'.[27] This categorical imperative defines the limits of a domain which must remain absolutely beyond the disposition of others. The 'infinite dignity' of each person consists in his claim that all others should respect the inviolability of this domain of free will.

Yet the concept of 'human dignity' does not acquire any systematic importance in Kant; the complete burden of justification is instead borne by the moral-philosophical explanation of autonomy: 'Autonomy is therefore the ground of the dignity of human nature and of every rational nature'.[28] Before we can understand

---

[26] Ernst Böckenförde, *Geschichte der Rechts- und Staatsphilosophie* (Tübingen: Mohr Siebeck, 2002), pp. 312–70.

[27] Immanuel Kant, *Groundwork of the Metaphysics of Morals*, ed. and trans. Mary Gregor (Cambridge: Cambridge University Press, 1997), p. 41 (Ak. 4:433).

[28] Ibid., p. 43 (Ak. 4:436).

what 'human dignity' means we have to make sense of the 'kingdom of ends'.[29] In the *Doctrine of Right*, Kant introduces human rights – or rather the 'sole' right to which everyone can lay claim in virtue of his humanity – by direct reference to the freedom of each 'insofar as it can coexist with the freedom of every other in accordance with a universal law'.[30] In Kant, too, human rights derive their moral content, which they spell out in the language of positive laws, from a universalistic and individualistic conception of human dignity. However, the latter is assimilated to an intelligible freedom beyond space and time and loses precisely those connotations of status which qualified it as the conceptual link between morality and human rights in the first place. Thus the point of the legal character of human rights gets lost, namely that they protect a human dignity that derives its connotations of self-respect and social recognition from a status in space and time – that of democratic citizenship.[31]

We have gathered together three elements from the perspective of conceptual history, namely, a highly moralized concept of human dignity, the recollection of a

[29] 'In the kingdom of ends everything has either a *price* or a *dignity*. What has a price can be replaced by something else as its *equivalent*; what on the other hand is raised above all price and therefore admits of no equivalent has a dignity'. Ibid., p. 42 (Ak. 4:434).

[30] Immanuel Kant, *Metaphysics of Morals*, ed. and trans. Mary Gregor (Cambridge: Cambridge University Press, 1996), p. 30 (Ak. 6:237).

[31] On the premises of Kant's own theory, such a 'mediation' between the transcendental realm of freedom and the phenomenal realm of necessity is neither necessary nor possible. But once the character of the free will is detranscendentalized (as it is in the theory of communicative action), the distance between morality and law has to be bridged. This is precisely what is achieved by the status-dependent concept of human dignity.

traditional understanding of social dignity and, with the emergence of modern law, the self-confident attitude of the legal person who makes claims against other legal persons. We would now have to make the transition from conceptual history to social and political history in order to render at least plausible the dynamic through which the contents of rational morality merged with the form of positive law through a generalization of the originally status-bound 'dignity' into 'human dignity'. On this I would like to present something which is more an illustrative example than a cast-iron historical proof. The process of claiming and enforcing human rights was seldom a peaceful matter. Human rights are the product of violent and at times of revolutionary struggles for recognition.[32] We can form a retrospective conception of the militant situation in which the three conceptual elements might have become connected with each other in the minds of the first freedom fighters (let us say, the Levellers). Historical experiences of humiliation and degradation, which were already interpreted in the light of an egalitarian Christian understanding of human dignity, represented one motive for resistance. But now the political outrage could find expression in the language of positive law as the self-confident demand for universal rights. Perhaps this was already connected, recollecting the familiar concept of dignity associated with rank, with the expectation that such basic rights would justify a status of citizens who recognize each other as subjects of equal rights.

---

[32] See Axel Honneth, *The Struggle for Recognition: Moral Grammar of Social Conflicts*, trans. Joel Anderson (Cambridge: Polity, 1996).

(3) The militant origin can only partially explain the polemical character which human rights have retained to this day. It is also the fact that they are morally charged that lends these state-sanctioned rights their unsaturated character. This character explains why a provocative tension found its way into modern societies with the two late eighteenth-century constitutional revolutions. Of course, in the social realm there is always and everywhere a difference between norms and actual behaviour; however, the unprecedented event of a constitution-making practice gave rise to an entirely different, utopian gap in the temporal dimension. On the one hand, human rights could acquire the quality of enforceable rights only within a particular political community – that is, within a nation state. On the other hand, the universalistic claim to validity of human rights which points beyond all national boundaries could be redeemed only within an inclusive worldwide political community.[33] This contradiction would find a reasonable resolution only in a constitutionalized world society (which would not therefore necessarily have the characteristics of a world republic).[34] From the outset, a

---

[33] Albrecht Wellmer, 'Menschenrechte und Demokratie', in Gosepath and Lohmann, *Philosophie der Menschenrechte*, pp. 265–91; for an astute analysis of the implications of the lack of congruence between human and civil rights for the 'aliens' living in a constitutional state, see Erhard Denninger, '"Die Rechte der Anderen": Menschenrechte und Bürgerrechte im Widerstreit', *Kritische Justiz* 3 (2009): 226–38.

[34] On this, see my texts 'Remarks on legitimation through human rights', in *The Postnational Constellation: Political Essays*, trans. Max Pensky (Cambridge: Polity, 2004), pp. 113–29; 'Does the constitutionalization of international law still have a chance?', in *The Divided West*, pp. 115–93; and 'The constitutionalization of international law and the legitimation problems of a constitution for society', in *Europe: The Faltering Project*,

tension of exclusion and inclusion has existed between human rights and established civil rights which under favourable historical conditions can trigger a 'mutually reinforcing dynamic' (Lutz Wingert).

This is not to suggest a self-propelling dynamic. Increasing the protection of human rights within nation states, or impelling the global spread of human rights beyond national boundaries, has never been possible without social movements and political struggles, without dauntless resistance to oppression and degradation. The struggle to implement human rights continues today in our own countries, as well as, for example, in Iran and China, in parts of Africa, or in Russia, Bosnia or Kosovo. Whenever an asylum seeker is deported at an airport behind closed doors, whenever a ship carrying refugees capsizes on the crossing from Libya

pp. 109–30. The contradiction between civil and human rights cannot be resolved exclusively through the global spread of constitutional states combined with the 'right to have rights' demanded by Hannah Arendt (with the situation of the displaced persons at the end of the Second World War in mind) because classical international law leaves international relations in a 'state of nature'. The need for coordination in world society which has arisen in the meantime could be satisfied only by a 'cosmopolitan juridical condition' (in the contemporary, revised Kantian sense).

In this context I must clear up a serious misunderstanding in the introduction to the special issue *Symposium on Human Rights: Origins, Violations, and Rectifications* (vol. 40, no. 1, 2009, p. 2) of the journal *Metaphilosophy* (and in Andreas Follesdal's article 'Universal human rights as a shared political identity. Necessary? Sufficient? Impossible?', ibid., pp. 78–91, at pp. 85ff.). I am, of course, a long-standing defender of the thesis that the collective identity of democratic political communities can be extended beyond the borders of existing nation states, and I by no means share the reservations harboured by liberal nationalists in this regard. In developing my plea for a multilevel global constitutional system, I have offered different reasons for the thesis that a world government is neither desirable nor feasible.

to the Italian island of Lampedusa, whenever a shot is fired at the border fence between the United States and Mexico, we, the citizens of the West, confront one more troubling question. The first human rights declaration set a standard which inspires refugees, people who have been thrust into misery, and those who have been ostracized and insulted, a standard which can give them the assurance that their suffering is not a natural destiny. The translation of the first human right into positive law gave rise to a *legal duty* to realize exacting moral requirements which has become engraved into the collective memory of humanity.

Human rights constitute a *realistic* utopia insofar as they no longer paint deceptive images of a social utopia which guarantees collective happiness but anchor the ideal of a just society in the institutions of constitutional states themselves.[35] Of course, this context-transcending idea of justice also introduces a problematic tension into social and political reality. Even apart from the merely symbolic force of human rights in those 'façade democracies' we find in South America and elsewhere,[36] the human rights policy of the United Nations exhibits the contradiction between the spreading rhetoric of human rights, on the one side, and their misuse to legitimize the usual power politics, on the other. To be sure, the UN General Assembly promotes the *codification of human rights in international law*, for example by enacting human rights covenants. The *institutionalization* of

---

[35] Ernst Bloch, *Natural Law and Human Dignity*, trans. Dennis J. Schmidt (Cambridge, MA: MIT Press, 1987).

[36] Marcelo Neves, 'The symbolic forms of human rights', *Philosophy and Social Criticism* 33 (2007): 411–44.

human rights has also made progress – with the procedure of the individual petition, with the periodic reports on the human rights situation in particular countries, and above all with the creation of international courts such as the European Court of Human Rights, various war crimes tribunals, and the International Criminal Court. Most spectacular of all are the humanitarian interventions authorized by the Security Council in the name of the international community, sometimes even against the will of sovereign governments. However, these cases in particular reveal the problematic nature of the attempt to promote a world order which is institutionalized for the present only in fragmentary ways. For what is worse than the failure of legitimate attempts is their ambiguity, which brings the moral standards themselves into disrepute.[37]

One need only recall the highly selective and shortsighted decisions of a non-representative and far from impartial Security Council, or the half-hearted and incompetent implementation of interventions which have been authorized – and their catastrophic failure (Somalia, Rwanda, Darfur). These supposed police

---

[37] Moreover, the currently prevailing 'gubernatorial human rights policy' is eroding the connection between human rights and democracy; on this, see Klaus Günther, 'Menschenrechte zwischen Staaten und Dritten', in connection with Ingeborg Maus, 'Menschenrechte als Ermächtigungsnormen internationaler Politik oder: der zerstörte Zusammenhang von Menschenrechten und Demokratie'; on this trend, see also Klaus Günther, 'Von der gubernativen zur deliberativen Menschenrechtspolitik: Die Definition und Fortentwicklung der Menschenrechte als Akt kollektiver Selbstbestimmung', in Gret Haller, Klaus Günther and Ulfrid Neumann (eds), *Menschenrechte und Volkssouveränität in Europa: Gerichte als Vormund der Demokratie?* (Frankfurt am Main: Campus, 2011), pp. 45–60.

operations continue to be conducted like wars in which the military write off the death and suffering of innocent civilians as 'collateral damage' (as in Kosovo). The intervening powers have yet to demonstrate in a single case that they are capable of marshalling the necessary energy and stamina for state-building – in other words, for reconstructing the destroyed or dilapidated infrastructure in the pacified regions (Afghanistan). When human rights policy becomes a mere fig leaf and vehicle for imposing major power interests, when the superpower flouts the UN Charter and arrogates to itself a right of intervention, and when it conducts an invasion in violation of humanitarian international law and justifies this in the name of universal values, this reinforces the suspicion that the programme of human rights *consists in* its imperialist misuse.[38]

---

[38] Carl Schmitt was the first to formulate this suspicion explicitly. See Carl Schmitt, *War/Non-War?*; Schmitt, *Das internationalrechtliche Verbrechen des Angriffskrieges und der Grundsatz 'Nullum crimen, nullapoena sine lege'*, ed. with notes and an afterword by Helmut Quaritsch (Berlin: Duncker & Humblot, [1945] 1994). Schmitt denounced human rights above all as the ideology which incriminates war as a legitimate means for resolving international conflicts. He already made the pacifist ideal of Wilsonian peace policy responsible for the fact 'that the distinction between just and unjust wars is giving rise to an ever deeper and sharper, ever more "total" distinction between friend and foe' (*War/Non-War?*, p. 50). In the brutish domain of international relations, he argued, the moralization of enemies constitutes a disastrous method for obscuring one's own interests; for the attacker barricades himself behind the apparently transparent façade of a purportedly rational, because humanitarian, abolition of war. The critique of a 'moralization' of law in the name of human rights is otiose, however, because it misses the point, namely the transposition of moral contents into the medium of coercive law. Insofar as the prohibition of war actually leads to the legal domestication of international relations, the distinction between 'just' and 'unjust' wars, whether based on natural law or religion, is superseded by 'legal' wars

97

The tension between idea and reality which was imported into reality itself as soon as human rights were translated into positive law confronts us today with the challenge to think and act realistically without betraying the utopian impulse. This ambivalence can lead us all too easily into the temptation either to align ourselves in an idealistic, but non-committal, way with the exacting moral requirements, or to adopt the cynical pose of the so-called realists. Since it is no longer realistic to follow Carl Schmitt in entirely rejecting the programme of human rights whose subversive force has in the meantime permeated the pores of *all* regions throughout the world, today 'realism' exhibits a different aspect. The direct unmasking critique is being replaced by a mild, deflationary one. This new minimalism relaxes the claim of human rights by cutting them off from their essential moral thrust, the protection of the equal dignity of every human being.

Following John Rawls, Kenneth Baynes contrasts this approach as a 'political' conception of human rights[39] with natural law notions of 'inherent' rights which every person is supposed to possess by his very human nature: 'Human rights are understood as conditions for inclusion in a political community'.[40] I agree with that. The problematic move is the next one which effaces the

which must then assume the form of global police measures. On this, see Klaus Günther, 'Kampf gegen das Böse? Zehn Thesen wider die ethische Aufrüstung der Kriminalpolitik', *Kritische Justiz* 27 (1994): 135–57.

[39] Kenneth Baynes, 'Toward a political conception of human rights', *Philosophy and Social Criticism* 35/3 (2009): 371–90.

[40] Kenneth Baynes, 'Discourse ethics and the political conception of human rights', *Ethics and Global Policy* 2/1 (2009): 1–21.

moral meaning of this inclusion, namely that everyone is respected in his human dignity as a subject of equal rights. Caution is certainly required in view of the disastrous failures of human rights policy. However, the latter do not provide sufficient reason for stripping human rights themselves of their moral surplus and restricting the focus of the topic of human rights from the beginning to questions of *international* politics.[41] This minimalism forgets that the still-persisting tensions between universal human rights and particular civil rights *at the domestic level* provide the normative reason for the international dynamic.[42] If we ignore this connection, the global spread of human rights requires a separate justification. This is provided by the argument that, in international relations, moral obligations between states (and citizens) first arise out of the growing systemic interconnectedness of an increasingly interdependent world society.[43] From this perspective, claims

---

[41] 'Human rights are understood primarily as international norms that aim to protect fundamental human interests and/or secure for individuals the opportunity to participate as members in political society' (ibid., p. 7).

[42] For a critique of this minimalist position, see Rainer Forst, 'The justification of human rights and the basic right to justification: a reflexive approach', *Ethics* 120 (2010): 711–40. There he writes: 'It is generally misleading to emphasize the political-legal function of such rights within international law (or political practice) of providing reasons for a politics of legitimate intervention. For this is to put the cart before the horse. We first need to construct (or find) a justifiable set of human rights that a legitimate political authority has to respect and guarantee, and then we will ask what kinds of legal structures are required at the international level to oversee this and help to ensure that political authority is exercised in that way' (p. 726). That said, the narrow view on international relations outlined suggests the notion of a paternalistic export of human rights which the West confers on the rest of the world.

[43] Joshua Cohen, 'Minimalism about human rights: the most we can hope for?', *Journal of Political Philosophy* 12 (2004): 190–213.

to inclusion arise first out of reciprocal dependencies in *factually* established interactions.[44] This argument has a certain explanatory force for the empirical question of how a responsiveness develops in our affluent societies to the legitimate claim of marginalized and underprivileged sections of the population who want to be included in liberal social conditions. However, these normative claims themselves are grounded in universalistic moral notions that have long since gained entry into the human and civil rights of democratic constitutions through the status-bound idea of human dignity. Only this *internal* connection between human dignity and human rights gives rise to the explosive fusion of moral contents with the medium of law in which the construction of just political orders must be performed.

This investing of the law with a moral charge is a legacy of the constitutional revolutions of the eighteenth century. To neutralize this tension would be to abandon the dynamic understanding which makes the citizens of our own, halfway liberal societies open to an ever more exhaustive realization of existing rights and to the ever-present acute danger of their erosion.

---

[44] 'Rights and corresponding duties are created by the special relationship that individuals stand in to one another, rather than as claims individuals have "simply in virtue of their humanity".' Kenneth Baynes, 'Toward a political conception of human rights', p. 382.

Appendix: The Europe of the Federal Republic

The interview with Thomas Assheuer (I) was conducted after the collapse of Lehman Brothers and a couple of days before the anticipated election of Barack Obama as president of the United States, with which great hopes were associated. Themes are already struck in the interview which I have now taken up and elaborated upon in my essay on the European constitution. With the outbreak of the financial crisis at the time, the calls by Nicolas Sarkozy and Jean-Claude Juncker for a joint European response of the EMU countries were opposed by Angela Merkel and Peer Steinbrück at the decisive meeting in Paris. This clearly foreshadowed the reaction pattern of national unilateralism.

I wrote the article that follows for *Die Zeit* (II) in response to the historic late-night meeting of 8–9 May 2010 at which Angela Merkel was overtaken by the force of the financial markets. She had struck the wrong balance between the inevitable aid for an over-indebted Greece and the opportunistic tactical manoeuvrings of domestic politics (in this case, the state elections in

101

North Rhine-Westphalia which were in any case a lost cause), and, after long weeks of hesitation, she had to submit meekly to the increasingly costly imperatives of the market. This was when the realization hit home to me for the first time that the failure of the European project was a real possibility.

Finally, the chance coincidence of the resolution on a 'pact for Europe' in Brussels with the coalition government of Christian democrats and liberals being elected out of office in the state of Baden-Württemberg provided the occasion for an intervention published in the *Süddeutschen Zeitung* (III). In the article, I contrasted the faceless exercise of rule behind closed doors by the European Council with the democratic success of a noisy, broad-based social movement. For the spectacular about turn of the German federal government in atomic energy policy overshadowed the momentous significance of a reversal in European policy executed on the quiet. The federal government had abandoned its faith in the infallibility of automatic 'mechanisms' in economic policy and initiated the change of course to a model of politicized intergovernmentalism by the heads of the euro club operating out of public view.

I After the bankruptcy: an interview

DIE ZEIT: Herr Habermas, the international financial system has collapsed and a global economic crisis is looming. What do you find most worrying about this?

JÜRGEN HABERMAS: What worries me most is the scandalous social injustice that the most vulnerable

102

social groups will have to bear the brunt of the social-ized costs for the market failure. The mass of those who are in any case not among the winners of glo-balization will now have to pick up the tab for the impacts on the real economy of a predictable dysfunc-tion of the financial system. Unlike the shareholders, they will not pay in money values but in the hard currency of their daily existence. On a global scale, this avenging fate is also afflicting the economically weakest countries. That's the political scandal. Yet pointing a finger at scapegoats strikes me as hypo-critical. The speculators were also acting consistently within the established legal framework in accordance with the socially recognized logic of profit maximiza-tion. Politics turns itself into a laughing stock when it resorts to moralizing instead of relying upon the enforceable law of the democratic legislator. Politics, and not capitalism, is responsible for promoting the common good.

ZEIT: You recently lectured at Yale University. Which images of this crisis left the deepest impression?

HABERMAS: A seemingly endless loop of melancholic Hopperian images of long rows of abandoned houses in Florida and elsewhere, with 'Foreclosure' signs on their front lawns, flickered across the television screens. Then you saw buses arriving with curious prospective buyers from Europe and wealthy Latin Americans, followed by the real-estate agent show-ing them the closets in the bedroom smashed in a fit of rage and despair. After my return I was struck by the sharp contrast between the agitated mood in the United States and the calm feeling of 'business as usual' here in Germany. In the US, the very real economic anxieties coincided with the hot end spurt of one of the most momentous election campaigns in recent memory. The crisis also instilled a more acute awareness of their personal interests in broad sectors of the electorate. It forced them to make decisions which were, if not necessarily more reasonable, then at least more rational – at any rate by comparison with the previous presidential election, which was ideologically polarized by 9/11. America will owe its first black president, if I may hazard a prediction on the eve of the election, and hence a major historical watershed in the history of its political culture, to this fortunate coincidence. Beyond this, however, the crisis could also be the harbinger of a changed political climate in Europe.

ZEIT: What do you have in mind?

HABERMAS: Such tidal shifts change the parameters of public discussion and, in the process, alter the spectrum of political alternatives regarded as possible. The Korean War marked the end of the New Deal, whereas Reagan and Thatcher and the waning of the Cold War marked the end of the era of social welfare programmes. Today, with the end of the Bush era and the bursting of the last neoliberal rhetorical balloons, the Clinton and New Labour programmes have run their course too. What is coming next? My hope is that that the neoliberal agenda will no longer be accepted at face value but will be opened to challenge. The whole programme of an unscrupulous subordination of the lifeworld to the imperatives of the market must be subjected to scrutiny.

ZEIT: For neoliberals the state is just one player in the economic field and should play as small a role as possible. Is this way of thinking now discredited?

HABERMAS: That depends on what course the crisis takes, on the perceptual capacities of the political parties and on the issues which find their way onto the public agenda. In Germany, at any rate, the situation is strangely becalmed. The agenda which recklessly prioritizes shareholder interests and is indifferent to increasing social inequality, to the emergence of an underclass, to child poverty, to a low wage sector, and so on, has been discredited. With its mania for privatization, this agenda hollows out the core functions of the state, it sells off the remnants of a deliberating public sphere to profit-maximizing financial investors, and it subordinates culture and education to the interests and moods of sponsors who are dependent on market cycles.

ZEIT: Are the consequences of the privatization mania now becoming apparent in the financial crisis?

HABERMAS: In the United States the crisis is exacerbating the already apparent material, moral, social and cultural damage caused by a policy of deregulation pushed to an extreme by the Bush administration. The privatization of social security and of health care, of public transport, of the energy supply, of the penal system, of military security services, of large sectors in school and university education, and the surrender of the cultural infrastructure of cities and communities to the commitment and generosity of private sponsors are part of a social design whose risks and consequences are difficult to reconcile with the egalitarian principles of a social and democratic constitutional state.

ZEIT: State agencies are simply incapable of conducting business in accordance with economic imperatives.

HABERMAS: Yes, but certain vulnerable areas of life should not be exposed to the risks of stock market speculation, a requirement which is not consistent with switching investments intended to provide for old age and retirement benefits to shares. In democracies there are also some public goods, for example undistorted political communication, which cannot be tailored to the profit expectations of financial investors. The citizens' need for information cannot be met by the culture of easily digestible sound bites which flourishes in a media landscape dominated by commercial television.

ZEIT: Are we experiencing a 'legitimation crisis' of capitalism, to quote the title of a controversial book of yours?

HABERMAS: Since 1989–90 it has become impossible to break out of the universe of capitalism; the only remaining option is to civilize and tame the capitalist dynamic from within. Even during the postwar period, the Soviet Union was not a viable alternative for the majority of the left in Western Europe. This is why in 1973 I wrote on legitimation problems 'in' capitalism. These problems have forced themselves onto the agenda once again, with greater or lesser urgency depending on the national context. A symptom of this is the demands for caps on managers' salaries and the abolition of 'golden parachutes', the outrageous compensation payments and bonuses.

After the bankruptcy

ZEIT: But aren't such policies merely window dressing? There are elections coming up next year.

HABERMAS: Yes, this is of course symbolic politics designed to divert attention away from the failures of the politicians and their economic consultants. They have long been aware of the need to regulate the financial markets. I just re-read Helmut Schmidt's crystal-clear article 'Beaufsichtigt die neuen Großspekulanten' ['Regulate the new mega-speculators'] from February 2007 (*Die Zeit*, no. 30). Everyone knew what was going on. But in America and Great Britain the political elites viewed the wild speculation as useful as long as things were going well. And Europe succumbed to the Washington Consensus. Here, too, there was a broad coalition of the willing for which Mr Rumsfeld didn't need to drum up support.

ZEIT: The Washington Consensus was the notorious economic plan drawn up by the IMF and the World Bank in 1990 through which first Latin America and then half of the world was supposed to be reformed. Its central promise was 'trickle-down'. Let the rich become richer and affluence will trickle down to the poor.

HABERMAS: Empirical evidence of the falsehood of this prognosis has been accumulating for many years. The effects of the increase in affluence are so asymmetrical, both at the national and at the global level, that the zones of poverty have grown before our very eyes.

ZEIT: Let's do a bit of reckoning with history [*Vergangenheitsbewältigung*]: Why is the affluence so unequally distributed? Did the end of the communist threat strip Western capitalism of its inhibitions?

HABERMAS: The form of capitalism reined in by nation states and by Keynesian economic policies – which, after all, conferred historically unprecedented levels of prosperity on the OECD countries – came to an end somewhat earlier, with the abandonment of the system of fixed exchange rates and with the oil crisis. The economic theory of the Chicago School acquired practical influence already under Reagan and Thatcher. This merely continued under Clinton and New Labour – and during the period of our most recent hero, Gordon Brown, as British finance minister. However, the collapse of the Soviet Union led to a fatal triumphalism in the West. The feeling of being among the winners of world history is seductive. In this case it inflated a theory of economic policy into a worldview permeating all areas of life.

ZEIT: Neoliberalism is a form of life. All citizens are supposed to become entrepreneurs and customers . . .

HABERMAS: . . . and competitors. The stronger, who win out in the free-for-all of the competitive society, can claim this success as their personal merit. It is deeply comical how managers – though not they alone – fall prey to the absurd elitist rhetoric of our talk shows, let themselves be celebrated in all seriousness as role models and mentally position themselves above the rest of society. It's as if they could no longer appreciate the difference between functional elites and the pompous ascriptive elites of early modern social estates. What, pray tell, is so admirable about the character and mentality of people in leadership

108

positions who do their job in a half-way competent manner? Another alarm signal was the Bush Doctrine announced in autumn 2002, which laid the groundwork for the invasion of Iraq. Since then the social Darwinist potential of market fundamentalism has become apparent not just in social policy but also in foreign policy.

ZEIT: But Bush wasn't alone. He was flanked by an impressive horde of influential intellectuals.

HABERMAS: Many of whom have learned nothing in the meantime. In the case of leading neoconservative thinkers like Robert Kagan, the thinking in terms of predatory categories à la Carl Schmitt has become if anything more apparent since the Iraq disaster. His recent commentary on the current regression of international politics into an increasingly unrestrained power struggle among adversaries armed with nuclear weapons is: 'The world has returned to normal'.

ZEIT: But looking back once again: What went wrong at the political level after 1989? Did capital simply become too powerful vis-à-vis politics?

HABERMAS: It became clear to me during the 1990s that politics must build up its capacities for joint action at the supranational level if it is to catch up with the markets. It even seemed that initial steps were being taken in this direction during the early part of the decade. George Bush the elder spoke in programmatic terms of a New World Order and seemed to want to make use of the long blocked – and ridiculed! – United Nations. At first there was a sharp increase in the number of humanitarian interventions enacted by the Security Council. The politically intended economic globalization should have been followed by a system of global political coordination and by a further legal codification of international relations. But the first ambivalent efforts already lost momentum under Clinton. The current crisis is again drawing attention to this deficiency. Since the beginning of the modern era, the market and politics have had to be repeatedly balanced off against each other in order to preserve the network of relations of solidarity among the members of political communities. There always remains a tension between capitalism and democracy because the market and politics rest on conflicting principles. The flood of decentralized individual choices unleashed within more complex networks also calls for regulations after the latest phase of globalization, something which cannot happen without a corresponding extension of political procedures through which interests are generalized.

ZEIT: But what does this mean? You continue to support Kant's cosmopolitanism and you advocate Carl Friedrich von Weizsäcker's idea of a global domestic politics. Forgive me, but that sounds illusory. After all, you only have to look at the current state of the United Nations.

HABERMAS: I must admit that a reform of the core institutions of the United Nations from the ground up would not go far enough. To be sure, the Security Council, the secretariat, the tribunals, and the powers and procedures of these institutions in general must be made fit for a global implementation of human rights and for the effective prohibition of violence as a matter of urgency – which is in itself an immense task.

After the bankruptcy

However, even if the United Nations Charter could be developed into a kind of constitution for the international community, this framework would still lack a forum in which the militarized struggle of the major powers would be transformed into institutionalized negotiations concerning the problems of the global economy in need of regulation, including problems of climate and environmental policy, of the distribution of contested energy resources, of scarce supplies of drinking water, and so on. At this transnational level problems of distribution arise which cannot be dealt with in the same way as violations of human rights or infringements of international security – ultimately as prosecutable offences – but have to be worked out through political negotiations.

ZEIT: But an institution responsible for this already exists, the G-8.

HABERMAS: That's an exclusive club in which some of these issues are discussed in a non-committal way. As it happens, there is a revealing discrepancy between the overhyped expectations associated with these events and the meagre results of the media spectacles, which remain without consequences. The illusory weight of expectation shows that the populations are very well aware – perhaps even more acutely aware than their own governments – of the unresolved problems of a future global domestic politics.

ZEIT: The talk of 'global domestic politics' sounds more like the dreams of a ghost-seer.

HABERMAS: Just few days ago most people would have regarded what is happening today as unrealistic. The European and Asian governments are outdoing each other with regulatory proposals to rectify deficiencies in the institutionalization of the financial markets. Even the SPD and the CDU are presenting proposals on accounting rules and capital adequacy ratios, on the personal liability of managers, on improved transparency and oversight of the stock market, and so on. Of course, a tax on stock market transactions, which would already go some of the way towards a global tax policy, is rarely mentioned. The new 'architecture of the financial system' announced with much fanfare will in any event be difficult to implement against US resistance. As to whether it would even go far enough given the complexity of these markets and the worldwide interdependence of the most important functional systems . . . International treaties, which is what the parties currently have in mind, can be revoked at any time. They cannot provide the basis for a watertight regime.

ZEIT: Even if new powers were transferred to the International Monetary Fund, that would not amount to a global domestic politics.

HABERMAS: I don't want to make predictions. Given the scale of the problems, the most we can do is to think about constructive proposals. The nation states must come to see themselves increasingly as members of the international community – even in their own interest. That is the most difficult task to be tackled over the next couple of decades. When we speak of 'politics' with an eye to the international stage, we often have in mind the actions of governments which have inherited the self-understanding of collective actors who make sovereign decisions. Today, however, this

112

self-understanding of the state as a Leviathan, which developed from the seventeenth century onwards in tandem with the European system of states, has already lost its continuity. The substance and composition of what we used to call 'politics' in the international arena is changing from one day to the next.

ZEIT: But how does this cohere with the social Darwinism in international relations which, as you claim, has experienced a resurgence on the global stage since 9/11?

HABERMAS: Perhaps we should take a step back and consider a somewhat larger context. Since the late eighteenth century, law has gradually permeated the politically constituted power of government and stripped it of the substantive character of mere 'force' in the domestic sphere. In its external relations, however, the state has preserved enough of this substance, in spite of the growth of intertwined international organizations and in spite of the increasingly binding power of international law. The concept of the 'political' shaped by the nation state is nevertheless in a state of flux. Within the European Union, for example, the member states continue to enjoy their monopoly on legitimate force while nevertheless implementing the laws enacted at the supranational level more or less without demur. This transformation of law and politics is also bound up with a capitalist dynamics which can be described in terms of a periodic interplay between a functionally driven opening followed in each case by a socially integrative closure at a higher level.

ZEIT: The market breaks open society and the welfare state closes it up again?

HABERMAS: The welfare state is a late and, as we are now learning, fragile accomplishment. Expanding markets and communications networks have always had an explosive force with simultaneously individualizing and liberating consequences for individual citizens; but each of these breaches has been followed by a reorganization of the old relations of solidarity within a more comprehensive institutional framework. This process began during the early modern period as, in the new territorial states, the ruling estates of the High Middle Ages were progressively parliamentarized, as in England, or mediatized by absolute monarchs, as in France. The process continued in the wake of the eighteenth- and nineteenth-century constitutional revolutions and of the twentieth-century welfare state legislative programmes. This legal taming of the Leviathan and class antagonism within civil society was no small matter. For the same functional reasons, however, this successful constitutionalization of state and society points today – after a further phase of economic globalization – to the constitutionalization of international law and of the strife-torn world society.

ZEIT: What role does Europe play in this optimistic scenario?

HABERMAS: Not the one it has actually played in the crisis. It is not clear to me why the recent crisis management of the European Union is being praised so highly. Gordon Brown was able to bring the American finance minister Paulsen to reinterpret the laboriously negotiated bail-out with his memorable decision because he brought the most important players in the euro zone on board through the mediation of the French president and against the initial resistance of Angela Merkel and her finance minister Peer Steinbrück. You need only examine this negotiation process and its outcome more closely. For it was after all the three most powerful nation states united in the EU who agreed, as sovereign actors, to coordinate their different measures – which happened to point in the same direction. In spite of the presence of Messrs Juncker and Barroso, the way this classical international agreement came about had almost nothing to do with a joint political will-formation of the European Union. The *New York Times* duly registered, not without a hint of malice, the Europeans' inability to agree upon a joint economic policy.

ZEIT: And to what do you attribute this inability?

HABERMAS: The present course of the crisis is revealing the flaw in the construction of the European Union: every country is responding with its own economic measures. Because the competences in the Union, simplifying somewhat, are divided up in such a way that Brussels and the European Court of Justice implement the economic freedoms while the resulting external costs are shunted off onto the member states, there is at present no joint will-formation at the level of economic policy. The most prominent member states are even divided over the principles governing how much state and how much market is desirable in the first place. Moreover, each country is conducting its own foreign policy, Germany first and foremost. The

115

Berlin Republic, for all its quiet diplomacy, is forgetting the lessons of history drawn by the old Federal Republic. The government is relishing the extended room for manoeuvre in foreign policy it has gained since 1989–90 and is falling back into the familiar pattern of national power politics between states, even though the latter have long ago shrunk to the format of minor princedoms.

ZEIT: And what should these princelings do?

HABERMAS: Are you asking me for my wish list? Under the present conditions, I regard graduated integration or different speeds of unification as the only possible scenario for overcoming the current paralysis of the EU. Thus Sarkozy's proposal for an economic government of the euro zone can serve as a starting point. This is not to imply that we would have to accept the statist background assumptions and protectionist intentions of its sponsor. Procedures and political results are two different things. The 'closer cooperation' in the field of economic policy would have to be followed by 'closer cooperation' in foreign policy. And neither could be conducted any longer through backroom deals behind the backs of the populations.

ZEIT: Even the SPD doesn't support this.

HABERMAS: The SPD leadership is abandoning this idea to the Christian Democrat Jürgen Rüttgers, the 'labour leader' in the Rhine and Ruhr region. All across Europe the social democratic parties have their backs to the wall because they are being forced to play zero-sum games with shrinking stakes. Why don't they grasp the opportunity to break out of their national cages and gain new room for manoeuvre at the European level? In this way they could even set themselves apart from the regressive competition from the left. Whatever 'left' and 'right' still mean today, only together could the euro zone countries acquire sufficient weight in world politics to be able to exert a reasonable influence on the agenda of the global economy. The alternative is to act as Uncle Sam's poodle and to throw themselves at the mercy of a global situation which is as dangerous as it is chaotic.

ZEIT: Speaking of Uncle Sam – you must be deeply disappointed with the United States. You envisaged the US as the draft horse of the new world order.

HABERMAS: Do we have any alternative to betting on this draft horse? The United States will emerge weakened from the current twofold crisis. But for the present it remains the liberal superpower, and it finds itself in a situation which encourages it to overhaul its neoconservative self-image as the paternalistic global benefactor. The worldwide export of its own form of life sprang from the false, centralized universalism of the old empires. By contrast, modernity rests upon the decentralized universalism of equal respect for everyone. It is in the interest of the United States not only to abandon its counterproductive stance towards the United Nations but to place itself at the head of the reform movement. Viewed historically, the confluence of four factors – superpower status, the oldest democracy in the world, the assumption of office of a, let's hope, liberal and visionary president, and a political culture in which normative impulses find an impressive resonance – represents an improbable constellation.

117

Today America is deeply distraught by the failure of the unilateral adventure, the self-destruction of neoliberalism and the abuse of its exceptionalist consciousness. Why shouldn't this nation, as it has done so often in the past, pull itself together and, before it is too late, try to bind the competing major powers of today – the global powers of tomorrow – into an international order which no longer needs a superpower? Why shouldn't an American president – buoyed by a watershed election – who finds that his scope for action in the domestic arena is severely restricted want to embrace this reasonable opportunity – this opportunity for reason – at least in foreign policy?

ZEIT: The so-called realists would dismiss your proposal with a jaded smile.

HABERMAS: I realize that many things speak against it. The new American president would have to overcome the resistance of the elites within his own party who are subservient to Wall Street; he would doubtlessly also have to be dissuaded from succumbing to the reflexes of a new protectionism. And the United States would need the friendly support of a loyal yet self-confident ally in order to undertake such a radical change in direction. A West which is 'bipolar' in a creative sense will become possible, of course, only when the EU learns to speak with one voice in foreign policy and, indeed, to use its internationally accumulated capital of trust to act in a farsighted manner itself. The 'Yes, but . . .' is obvious. Yet in times of crisis a somewhat broader perspective may be more needful than that offered by mainstream advice and the petty manoeuvring of politics as usual.

II   *The euro will decide the fate of the European Union*

These are fateful times. The West and Russia celebrated the anniversary of the victory over Nazi Germany on May 8 and 9, respectively. Here in Germany these are also officially known as 'days of liberation'. This year the armed forces of the Allied coalition against Germany (also including a Polish unit) marched together in the victory parade. Angela Merkel stood directly beside Vladimir Putin on Red Square. Her presence reaffirmed the spirit of a 'new' Germany: the postwar generations have not forgotten that they were also liberated by the Russian army – and that the Red Army in the process suffered the heaviest casualties.

The chancellor had flown in from Brussels, where, in an entirely different capacity, she had witnessed a defeat of a completely different kind. The picture of that press conference in which the EU heads of government announced their decision to establish a joint rescue fund for the ailing euro betrays the fretfulness, not of the 'new', but of present-day Germany. The grating photo captures the stony faces of Merkel and Nicolas Sarkozy – worn-out heads of government who had nothing left to say to each other. Is it destined to become the iconographic document of the demise of a vision that shaped postwar European history for over half a century?

In Moscow, Merkel stood in the shadow of the tradition of the old Federal Republic. But in Brussels on 8 May, Merkel had behind her the weeks of struggle of a hard-nosed lobbyist for the national interests of the economic powerhouse of the European Union. Appealing to

119

the model of German fiscal discipline, she had blocked a timely joint intervention by the EU to shore up Greece's creditworthiness against speculation aimed at triggering a state bankruptcy. Ineffectual declarations of intent had frustrated concerted preventive action – on the mistaken assumption that Greece was an isolated case.

Only after the most recent slump in the stock market did the chancellor relent meekly, her resistance broken down by the collective psychological massage administered by the presidents of the United States, the International Monetary Fund and the European Central Bank. Out of fear of the weapons of mass destruction wielded by the tabloid press, she seemed to have lost sight of the destructive force of the weapons of mass destruction wielded by the financial markets. She would hear nothing of a euro zone, about which the president of the European Commission, José Manuel Barroso, would declare in the days that followed: if you don't want a unified economic policy, you'll also have to forget about the monetary union.

The sea change

The momentousness of the Brussels decision of 8 May 2010 is now dawning on all concerned. The Anglicizing metaphors prevalent in Germany, which have us incessantly deploying 'rescue parachutes' and cobbling together 'rescue packages', should not conceal the fact that the hastily agreed-upon emergency measures to save the euro will have different consequences from those of any previous bail-out. Because the Commission is now taking out loans on the market for the European Union as a whole, this 'crisis mechanism' is a 'Community instrument' that changes the basis on which the European Union operates.

The fact that, from now on, the taxpayers of the euro zone bear joint liability for the budgetary risks of each of the other member states amounts to a paradigm shift. This brings a long-repressed problem to awareness. The financial crisis, which has developed into a crisis of the states, calls to mind the birth defect of an incomplete political union marooned in midstream. A common market with a partially shared currency has developed in an economic zone of continental proportions with a huge population, but without institutions being established at the European level capable of effectively coordinating the economic policies of the member states.

No one can write off any more the call by the president of the IMF for 'European economic governance' as unreasonable. The models of a 'rule-compliant' economic policy and a 'disciplined' budgetary policy that conform to the requirements of the stability pact do not meet the requirement of a flexible adaptation to rapidly shifting political constellations. Of course, the national budgets have to be balanced. But this is not just a matter of Greek 'cheating' and Spanish 'delusions of affluence' but of aligning levels of economic development within a currency area which includes diverse national economies. The stability pact, which France and Germany themselves suspended in 2005, has become a fetish. Imposing harsher sanctions will not be sufficient to offset the undesirable consequences of a planned asymmetry between the complete economic and the incomplete political unification of Europe.

The Europe of the Federal Republic

Even the business editors of the *Frankfurter Allgemeine Zeitung* see 'the European Union at a crossroads'. Of course, they are merely invoking a nightmare scenario to stir up Deutschmark nostalgia against the so-called soft currency countries, while a pliable chancellor is suddenly speaking of the need for Europeans to become 'more tightly intermeshed economically and financially'. But there is not the slightest hint of an awareness of a sea change. Some are blurring the causal connection between the euro crisis and the banking crisis and are blaming deficient fiscal discipline for the entire disaster. The others are eagerly trying to talk down the problem of the overdue harmonization of national economic policies into a matter of better management.

The European Commission intends to put the interim rescue fund for the euro on a permanent footing and to vet national budgets – even before they are submitted to the national parliaments. It is not that these proposals are unreasonable. However, it is outrageous to suggest that such an encroachment by the Commission on budgetary prerogatives of the national parliaments would not impinge on the treaties and that it would not represent an unprecedented exacerbation of the long-standing democratic deficit. An effective coordination of economic policies must involve an increase in the powers of the parliament in Strasbourg; it will also stimulate the need for better coordination in other policy fields.

The euro zone countries are heading towards a situation in which they will have to choose between a deepening of European cooperation and relinquishing the euro. It is a matter not of 'mutual surveillance of economic policies' (Jean-Claude Trichet), but of concerted action. And German politics is woefully unprepared for that.

The new generation and the new indifference
After the Holocaust, it took decades of concerted efforts – from Adenauer and Heinemann, through Brandt and Helmut Schmidt, to Weizsäcker and Kohl – to bring the Federal Republic back into the fold of civilized nations. A tactically astute Genscherism and an opportunistic orientation to the West were not enough. What was needed was an infinitely arduous change in mentality on the part of the entire population. What ultimately won over our European neighbours were, first and foremost, the changed normative convictions and the liberal-minded attitudes of the younger generations who had grown up in the Federal Republic. And, of course, the fact that the convictions of the politicians active at that time could be relied upon played a decisive role in diplomatic relations.

The historically justified distrust of the Germans could not be weakened by their discernible interest in a peaceful European unification alone. West Germans seemed to have to come to terms with the partition of the country in any case. Mindful of their past nationalistic excesses, they could have no difficulty in forgoing the recovery of sovereignty rights, in accepting the role of the largest net contributor to Europe and, if need be, in making concessions that, in any case, paid off for the Federal Republic. To be convincing, the German commitment had to be normatively anchored. Jean-Claude Juncker gave an apt description of the stress test when, with an eye to Angela Merkel's cool interest calculation,

123

he discerned an unwillingness 'to take domestic political risks for Europe'.

The new German intransigence has deeper roots. In the wake of reunification, Germany's perspective had already changed as an enlarged country preoccupied with its own problems. But there was a more sweeping change in mentalities after Helmut Kohl. With the exception of a too quickly exhausted Joschka Fisher, since Gerhard Schröder took office a normatively unambitious generation has been in power which has become preoccupied with a short-winded approach to the day-to-day problems of an increasingly complex society. Conscious of the diminishing room for political manoeuvre, these people shy away from farsighted goals and constructive political projects, let alone an undertaking like European unification.

The current German elites are enjoying the return to normality as a nation state. Having reached the end of a 'long path to the West', they are certified democrats and can once again be 'just like the others'. What has disappeared is the anxiousness of a people who were also morally defeated and were compelled to engage in self-criticism, to find their bearings more rapidly in the postnational constellation. In a globalized world everyone has to learn to incorporate the perspectives of others into his or her own instead of withdrawing into an egocentric blend of aestheticization and utility maximization. One political symptom of the dwindling willingness to learn are the Maastricht and Lisbon verdicts of the German Federal Constitutional Court, which cling to outmoded dogmatic legal conceptions of sovereignty. The solipsistic and normatively depleted mindset of this self-absorbed colossus in the middle of Europe can no longer even guarantee that the EU will survive in its unstable status quo.

The blunted sense of crisis

In and of itself, a change in mentality is no reason for reproach; but the new indifference has implications for our political perceptions of the challenges ahead. Who is really willing to learn the lessons from the banking crisis so eloquently enshrined in the declarations of intent of the G-20 summit in London over a year ago – and to fight for them?

When it comes to taming a financial capitalism spinning out of control, there can be no doubt about the majority preferences among the national populations. In autumn 2008, for the first time in the history of capitalism, the backbone of the financial market-driven global economic system could be rescued from the brink of collapse only by the guarantees of the taxpayers. And the fact that capitalism is no longer able to reproduce itself under its own steam has now taken root in the consciousness of citizens who, as taxpayers, must bear liability for the 'system failure'.

The demands of the experts are on the table. Among the proposals under discussion are increasing the equity capital of the banks, greater transparency for the activities of hedge funds, improved oversight of stock markets and rating agencies, the prohibition of fanciful but economically destructive speculative instruments, a tax on financial transactions, a bank levy, the separation of investment from commercial banking, and the precautionary break-up of banking conglomerates that are 'too big to fail'. A certain nervousness was discernible on the face of Josef Ackermann, the shrewd head lobbyist of the banking industry, when the television presenter Maybrit Illner invited him to choose among at least a selection of these legislative 'instruments of torture'.

I don't mean to suggest that regulating the financial markets would be a straightforward matter. It certainly also requires the expertise of the shrewdest bankers. But the good intentions are thwarted not so much by the 'complexity of the markets' as by the timidity and lack of independence of the national governments. They are thwarted by the rash renunciation of any international cooperation aimed at constructing the political capacities for joint action that we lack – worldwide, in the European Union and, to begin with, within the euro zone. When it comes to the bail-out for Greece, currency dealers and speculators are more inclined to believe Ackermann's shrewd defeatism than Merkel's lukewarm consent to the euro rescue fund; realistically, they don't think that the euro countries are capable of working together resolutely. How could it be otherwise in a club that squanders its energies in cockfights over appointments to its most influential posts – only to fill them with the most colourless figures?

In times of crisis, even individuals can write history. Our lame political elites, who prefer to read the tabloid headlines, must not use as an excuse that the populations are the obstacle to a deeper European unification. For they know best that popular opinion established by opinion polls is not the same thing as the outcome of a public deliberative process leading to the formation of a democratic will. To date there has not been a single

European election or referendum in any country that wasn't ultimately about national issues and tickets. We are still waiting for a single political party to undertake a constructive campaign to inform public opinion, to say nothing of the blinkered nationalistic vision of the left (by which I don't just mean the German party The Left).

With a little political backbone, the crisis of the single currency can bring about what some once hoped for from a common European foreign policy, namely a cross-border awareness of a shared European destiny.

III A pact for or against Europe?

The last week in March 2010 was dominated by two major political events. The loss of power of the governing parties in the state of Baden-Württemberg, the heartland of the CDU, set the seal on the federal government's decision to make a rapid withdrawal from atomic energy; and two days earlier the European Council had coupled its decisions on the stabilization of the single currency with a long overdue initiative aimed at coordinating the economic policies in the euro zone member states. The importance of this advance in integration policy is generating hardly any public attention, however, for in other respects the two events stand in striking contrast. In Baden-Württemberg a social movement, after forty years of civil society protest, overturned a tough mindset on which the industry-friendly elites were able to rely until now. In Brussels, after a year of speculation against the euro, a package of measures 'for economic governance' was adopted behind closed doors whose repercussions will occupy lawyers, economists and political scientists in the first instance. The change in mentality achieved through long-term grassroots struggles in the first case contrasts with an advance in integration in the cooperation among national governments under the short-term pressure of the financial markets in the second.

The reversal in energy policy, which has been on the horizon for decades in the political light of a vociferous, argumentative public sphere, represents a sea change. But is this also true of the political shift towards a more intensive coordination of policies which, according to the European treaty, fall under the national spheres of competence, a shift which was negotiated in an expertocratic manner, disappeared into the business sections of newspapers and was accomplished almost without comment? What is the problem here – and can it even be solved through an agreement among the heads of government of the member states involved?

The flaw in the construction of the monetary union
I leave to one side the technical financial question of whether the stability mechanism agreed upon in Brussels, which in 2013 will succeed the rescue fund concluded in May 2010, will put an end to the speculation against the euro. More important is the political question of the flaw in the construction of the monetary union which has been made clear to *everyone* by the speculation on the financial markets. When the euro was introduced in 1999, some of those involved still hoped that the process of *political* unification would

continue. Other proponents put their faith in the ordo-liberal textbook, which has more confidence in the economic constitution than in democracy. In their view, observing simple rules for consolidating the national budgets should be sufficient to bring economic development in the different countries (as measured by the unit labour costs) into alignment.

Both expectations have been dramatically disappointed. The financial, debt and euro crises occurring in rapid succession have revealed the flaw in the construction of a gigantic economic and currency area which lacks the necessary instruments to conduct a joint economic policy. These systemic constraints have forced Eurosceptics like Angela Merkel into taking a reluctant step in the direction of integration. The flaw is now supposed to be rectified through the informal mechanism of 'open coordination'. For the actors concerned, this expedient has the advantage of letting sleeping dogs lie. On the other hand, even assuming it works, it has undemocratic implications, and it is apt to stoke up mutual resentments among the populations of the various member states.

The heads of government have committed themselves to implementing a catalogue of financial, economic, social and wage policy measures in their respective countries which are actually matters for the national parliaments (or for the unions and management). The recommendations reflect a model of politics which bears a German imprint. I will not even discuss the wisdom of an economic policy whose austerity measures expose the countries on the periphery to the threat of a counterproductive permanent deflation. Instead I will concentrate on the procedure. Every year the heads of government propose to look over each other's shoulders to determine whether their colleagues have brought debt levels, the retirement age and labour market deregulation, the social benefits and health-care systems, public sector wages, the wage ratio, corporation tax and much else besides into conformity with the 'guidelines' of the European Council.

The wrong method

The legally non-binding character of the prior inter-governmental agreement on policies which encroach on the core competences of the member states and their parliaments gives rise to a dilemma. If the recommendations on economic governance remain ineffective, the problems this approach is supposed to solve are perpetuated. If, however, the governments in fact coordinate their measures in the manner envisaged they have to 'procure' the necessary legitimation for this at home. But that inevitably gives rise to a *claire-obscur* of gentle pressure from above and involuntary-voluntary accommodation from below. What is meant by the right of the Commission to examine the budgets of the member states 'in a timely manner', hence before the parliamentary decisions, if not the presumption of creating an effective precedent?

Behind this grey veil, the national parliaments (and, where they are involved, the unions) cannot avoid the suspicion of merely rubber-stamping prior decisions taken elsewhere – that is, merely reproducing them in a more concrete form. This suspicion inevitably corrodes any democratic credibility. The wishy-washy character of a mode of coordination whose legal status is deliberately left vague is not sufficient to support the regulations required for concerted action by the Union. Such decisions have to be legitimized along *both* of the paths foreseen for decisions of the Union – not only indirectly through the governments represented in the Council but also directly through the European Parliament. Otherwise the familiar centrifugal dynamic of finger-pointing at 'Brussels' is merely accelerated – in other words, the wrong method operates as a divisive force.

As long as the European citizens see their national governments as the only players on the European stage, they perceive the decision-making processes as a zero-sum game in which their own actors have to prevail against the others.

The national heroes compete with 'the others' who are to blame for all of the impositions and demands that the Brussels monster places on 'us'. Only by looking to the parliament in Strasbourg which they have elected, and which is composed along party lines and not according to nations, could the European citizens perceive the tasks of economic governance as tasks to be mastered in a cooperative manner.

And the alternative?

A more ambitious alternative would be if the Commission performed these functions in a democratic manner through the 'ordinary legislative procedure', hence with the agreement of the Council *and* the Parliament. However, that would require a transfer of competences from the member states to the Union, and such a drastic change in the treaty seems unrealistic for the time being.

It is probably correct that, *under present conditions*, the Europe-weary populations would reject a further transfer of sovereignty rights even in the core domains of the Union. But this prediction is too comfortable if the political elites use it as a pretext to shirk their responsibility for the wretched state of the Union. It should not be regarded as a matter of course that the decades-long broad-based support for European unification has decreased sharply even in Germany. Today the process of European unification, which was conducted above the heads of the population from the very beginning, has reached an impasse because it cannot proceed further without being switched from the established administrative mode to one involving increased popular participation. Instead of acknowledging this, the political elites are burying their heads in the sand. They are persisting unapologetically in their elite project and the disenfranchisement of the European citizens. I would like to present just three reasons for this impudence.

The rediscovery of the German nation state

The reunification spurred a change in mentality in Germany which (as studies in political science show) has also affected the self-interpretation and orientation of German foreign policy and lent it a more pronounced self-centred character. Since the 1990s, Germany has gradually adopted a self-confident image of itself as a militarily based 'medium-sized power' acting as a player on the global political stage. This self-understanding

132

is suppressing the culture of restraint cultivated up to that time which saw Germany as a civil power whose main aim was to contribute to the legal domestication of the system of unbridled competition between states. This transformation is also apparent in European policy, especially since the 2005 change of government. Hans-Dietrich Genscher's conception of the 'European vocation' of a cooperative Germany is steadily deteriorating into an undisguised leadership claim of a 'European Germany in a German Europe'. It is not as though the unification of Europe was not in Germany's interest from the beginning. But the consciousness of an obligating historical-moral inheritance supported diplomatic restraint and the willingness also to adopt the perspectives of others, to acknowledge the importance of normative viewpoints and on occasion to defuse conflicts through concessions.

In Angela Merkel's case, this may still play a role in dealings with Israel. But the primacy of national concerns was never made as nakedly apparent as by the steadfast resistance of the chancellor, who, before the debacle of 8 May 2010, blocked European aid for Greece and the rescue parachute for the euro for weeks on end. The current package has also been cobbled together by model students of economic policy with such a lack of sensitivity that the neighbouring countries will take the first opportunity to start pointing fingers at the 'German' policy model, which they don't want to have foisted upon them, instead of at 'Brussels'. As it happens, the Europe-hostile Lisbon judgement of the Federal Constitutional Court is also part of the new German mindset. By arbitrarily defining unalterable national spheres of competence, the Court is setting itself up as the protector of national identity against aspirations towards greater integration. Constitutional lawyers hit the nail on the head when they para-phrased the judgement sarcastically as 'The German Constitutional Court says "yes" to Germany'.

Demoscopic opportunism

The new German normality does not explain the fact that, to date, there has not been a single European elec-tion and hardly a single referendum in any member state which wasn't ultimately decided on national issues and tickets. Of course, political parties avoid thematiz-ing unpopular issues. On the one hand, this is trivial because the goal of parties must be to win elections. On the other hand, why European elections have been dominated for decades by issues and persons that were not even up for decision is a far from trivial question. The fact that the citizens fail to grasp the relevance of events in Strasbourg and Brussels which are subjectively felt to be distant means that the political parties do indeed have an obligation to inform, one which they nevertheless obstinately shirk.

To be sure, today politics in general seems to be developing towards an aggregate state marked by a renunciation of perspectives and creative drive. The increasing complexity of the matters in need of regu-lation forces politicians into short-winded reactions within shrinking scopes for action. As though politi-cians had adopted the unmasking perspective of systems theory, they are shamelessly following the opportunistic script of a pragmatic power politics guided by opinion polls which has shrugged off all normative commitments. Merkel's nuclear moratorium is only the most conspicuous example. And it was not the German minister of defence Guttenberg but the head of government herself who (in the words of the *Frankfurter Allgemeine Zeitung*) 'turned half of the Republic and almost the entire CDU into liars' when she kept the publicly exposed plagiarist in office in deference to his popularity. In a cynical calculation, she sold out the constitutional understanding of office for a few pieces of silver, which, at the end of the day, she was not able to collect at the ballot box. To top it all, the normality of the practice was confirmed by the full military honours shown the departing minister.

Underlying this is an understanding of democracy which the *New York Times*, after the re-election of George W. Bush, captured in the formula 'post-truth democracy'. By making its activity completely dependent on conformity with public moods to which it anxiously panders from one election date to the next, politics is eroding the meaning of the democratic process. The point of a democratic election is not merely to depict a contingent spectrum of opinion but to reflect the result of a process of public opinion-formation. The votes cast in the polling booth bear the institutional weight of democratic participation only in connection with the publicly articulated opinions which have been formed in the communicative exchange of issue-relevant positions, information and reasons. This is why the German Basic Law privileges the parties which, according to Article 21, 'participate in the formation of the political will of the people'. The European Union will not be able to acquire a democratic character either as long as the political parties are too timid *even to thematize* alternatives to decisions of great moment.

The discontent with the political and media class

The media are not merely passive spectators of the deplorable transformation of politics. On the one hand, the politicians allow themselves to be enticed by the gentle pressure of the media into short-winded forms of self-promotion. On the other hand, the programming of the media lets itself become infected by this impatient occasionalism. The cheerful moderators of the innumerable talk shows, with their never-changing line-ups of guests, serve up a mess of opinions which robs the last viewer of the hope that *reasons* could still *count* in political questions. Sometimes the ARD Press Club shows how it can be done better.

Granted, if I am not mistaken, our quality press does not cut such a bad figure in international comparisons. But even these leading media do not remain unaffected by the circumstance that the media are *coalescing with* the political classes – and are even proud of this accolade. An example is the disconcerting applause for the chancellor by the upmarket 'liberal' weekly when, in the *causa* Guttenberg, she subjected the political culture of the country to the Berlusconi treatment. Moreover, if the commentating press wanted to function as a counterbalance to a perspectiveless politics, it would not allow its themes to be dictated to it entirely by the rhythm of daily events. For example, it is treating the efforts to come to grips with the euro crisis as a highly specialized economic topic; but then the context is lacking when at long intervals the political editorial departments deign to address the implications of the crisis for reorganizing the European Union as a whole after all.

The rediscovery of the German nation state, the new mode of short-term politics without a compass, and the coalescing of politics and the media into a single class may explain why politics lacks the stamina for such a major project as European unification. But looking upwards at the political elites and the media may be to look in completely the wrong direction. Perhaps the motivations which are currently lacking can only come from below, from within civil society itself. The phase-out of atomic energy is an example of the fact that the things which are taken for granted in politics and culture, and hence the parameters of public discussion, do not change without the dogged, subterranean work of social movements.

Where are the motives supposed to come from?
A social movement for Europe is not in the air. Instead we are observing something else, a disenchantment with politics whose causes remain unclear. The customary diagnoses link the discontent with personality and stylistic traits of celebrated substitute and oppositional figures. It is reported that many citizens admire the lateral entrant into politics Joachim Gauck for his rough-hewn profile as a lifelong opposition figure, the communicator Guttenberg for the eloquence and brilliance of his elegant self-representation, and the moderator Heiner Geissler for his gnarled image as a congenial trickster – all of them colourful traits that the staid administrators of the political routine conspicuously lack. However,

this anti-political enthusiasm for figures above the parties could also be an outlet for an entirely different frustration – for exasperation with a politics *that makes too few demands.*

In earlier times, the policies of German governments had a clearly recognizable profile: Adenauer was preoccupied with the connection to the West, Brandt with Ostpolitik and the Third World; Schmidt relativized the fate of Europe by seeing it as a small part of the world economy and Helmut Kohl wanted to integrate the unified Germany into a unified Europe. All of them still wanted something! Already Schröder was someone who reacted rather than taking initiatives; at least Joschka Fischer wanted to bring about a decision on the *finalité*, or at any rate the direction, of European unification. Since 2005 the contours have dissolved completely. It is no longer discernible what is at stake, whether there is even still more at stake than the next electoral success. The citizens sense that a normatively hollowed-out politics is *withholding* something from them. This deficit finds expression both in the turning away from organized politics and in the new enthusiasm for grassroots protest, for which 'Stuttgart 21' is the cipher.[1] It might nevertheless be worthwhile for one or other of the political parties to roll up its sleeves and take the fight for European unification to the marketplaces.

Renouncing 'grand' projects is not enough. The

---

[1] This refers to the divisive public controversy and protests over the major public works project to replace the existing central railway station in Stuttgart with an underground station, which is scheduled to go ahead following a late 2011 referendum in the state of Baden-Württemberg (*Trans.*).

international community cannot shut its eyes to climate change, the worldwide risks of nuclear technology, the need to regulate financial market-driven capitalism and the implementation of human rights at the international level. And, by comparison with the scale of these problems, the task we have to perform in Europe is almost manageable.

Sources

The essay 'The concept of human dignity and the realistic utopia of human rights' was published in *Metaphilosophy* (41 [2010], pp. 464–80). It has been revised for this volume.

'After the bankruptcy', the interview conducted by Thomas Assheuer with Jürgen Habermas, originally appeared on 6 November 2008 in the German weekly *Die Zeit* (p. 53), and in translation under the title 'Afterword: Lessons of the Financial Crisis', in Jürgen Habermas, *Europe: The Faltering Project* (Cambridge: Polity, 2009, pp. 194–7).

The article 'The European Union must decide between transnational democracy and post-democratic executive federalism' originally appeared on 20 May 2010 in *Die Zeit* (p. 47).

'A pact for or against Europe?' originally appeared on 7 April 2011 in the *Süddeutschen Zeitung* (p. 11).